Sadlier WORD STUDY Reading

Level D

DISCARD

CURRICULUM COLLECTION

Senior Authors

Richard T. Vacca
Lesley Mandel Morrow

Contributing Authors

Charles T. Mangrum II, Ed.D.
Professor of Reading Education
University of Miami

Stephen S. Strichart, Ph.D.
Professor of Education
Florida International University

Program Consultants

Raymond P. Kettel, Ed.D.
Associate Professor of Education
University of Michigan
Dearborn, Michigan

Sylvia A. Rendón, Ph.D.
Coordinator for English Language Arts
Cypress-Fairbanks I.S.D.
Houston, Texas

Lisbeth Ceaser, Ph.D.
Dir., Precollegiate Academic Development
California Polytechnic State University
San Luis Obispo, California

Susan Stempleski, M.Ed., M.A.
Lecturer in TESOL
Teachers College, Columbia University
New York, New York

Sadlier-Oxford
A Division of William H. Sadlier, Inc.

Advisors

The publisher wishes to thank the following teachers and administrators who read portions of the series prior to publication for their comments and suggestions.

Rubbie D. Baker
Fifth Grade Teacher
Decatur, Georgia

Margarite K. Beniaris
Assistant Principal
Chicago, Illinois

Trish Bresch
Elementary School Teacher
Westmont, New Jersey

Shaun R. Burke
Fourth Grade Teacher
Rancho Santa Margarita,
California

Margaret Clifford
Principal
Michigan City, Indiana

Veronica Durden
Counselor
Beaumont, Texas

Christine Henschell
Sixth Grade Teacher
Grand Rapids, Michigan

Malini Horiuchi
Fifth Grade Teacher
Hollis Hills, New York

Amy T. Kwock
Principal
Honolulu, Hawaii

Connie Sartori
Sixth Grade L.A. Teacher
Seminole, Florida

Carmen Talavera
Fourth Grade Teacher
Long Beach, California

Acknowledgments

William H. Sadlier, Inc., gratefully acknowledges the following for the use of copyrighted materials:

Dictionary entries and pronunciation keys (text only). Reprinted from Macmillan School Dictionary 1, with the permission of the publisher, The McGraw-Hill Companies, Inc. Copyright © 1990 by Macmillan Publishing Company, a division of Macmillan, Inc.

"Everybody's Uncle Sam" (text only) by Lester David. By Permission of Maggie Rosen. Reprinted from BOYS' LIFE magazine (July 1996), published by Boy Scouts of America.

"It's Our World, Too!" (text only) from IT'S OUR WORLD, TOO! by Phillip Hoose. Copyright © 1993 by Phillip Hoose. Used by permission of Little, Brown and Company (Inc.).

"Meet an Underwater Explorer" (text only) by Luise Woelflein. Reprinted from the June 1994 issue of RANGER RICK magazine, with the permission of the publisher, the National Wildlife Federation. Copyright © 1994 by the National Wildlife Federation.

"Blazing a Twisted Trail" (text only). Reprinted from the October 25, 1996, issue of TIME FOR KIDS magazine, with the permission of the publisher, Time Inc. Copyright © 1996 Time Inc.

"Your Future in Space" (text only) by Alan L. Bean. By permission of the author. Reprinted from BOYS' LIFE magazine (July 1996), published by the Boy Scouts of America.

Photo Credits

ADVENTURE PHOTO & FILM/ Colin Monteath: 46 inset ARCHIVE: 64; American Stock: 105; ART RESOURCE: 34 ALAN L. BEAN: 174; BRIDGEMAN ART LIBRARY/ Royal Society, London, UK: 137; CORBIS: 53, 137, 140, 141, 147, 149, 152, 170, 171, 172, 175, 177 bottom; TempSport: 17 top right; Bettmann: 29, 30, 31, 39 bottom left & right, 45, 60 inset, 77, 103, 110, 112, 113, 113 top & bottom, 122, 162, 177 bottom, 203, 220; Historical Picture Archive: 35; Owen Franken: 41; Jeff Fanuga: 42; Niall MacLeod: 46 right; Wolfgang Kaehler: 48; George Lepp: 57; Philadelphia Museum of Art: 67; North Carolina Museum of Art/ Jacob Lawrence: 70; Hulton-Deutsch Collection: 81; Gregory Clements/Winslow Homer: 88; Ron Austing/Frank Lane Picture Agency: 94; Roger Ressmeyer: 128, 169; Sygma/ Les Stone: 132; Outline/ Timothy Greenfield-Sanders: 136; Paul A. Souders: 144; AFP: 184, 209 inset; Robert Maass: 191; Lake County Museum: 193; Joseph Sohm/ChromoSohm, Inc.: 204, 209; UPI: 208; Ted Spiegel: 214; Craig Lovell: 215; Catherine Karnow: 221 right DIGITAL VISION: 36 ADRIAN FISHER: 95 FPG/ Jim Cummins: 13; Vcg: 62 bottom right; Neil Nissing: 72; AL GIDDINGS: 61; THE GRANGER COLLECTION: 155, 157, 159; Currier & Ives: 91; THE IMAGE BANK: 150 left; Terje Rakke: 5; ActionPix, Inc.: 20; Per Eriksson: 43; THE IMAGE WORKS/ Esbin-Anderson: 75; Jeff Greenberg: 115; M. Greenlar: 118; Michelle Gabel: 134; Steve Rubin: 135; Peter Hvidzak: 177; Bob Daemmrich: 183, 199; J. Greenberg: 207; INDEX STOCK IMAGERY: 179, 222; NASA: 163, 173 right NATIONAL GEOGRAPHIC SOCIETY/ William R. Curtsinger: 31; 60 inset; Raymond Gehman: 68; Marie-Louise Brimberg: 84; Jodi Cobb: 87; Richard Nowitz: 93; PHOTODISC/ 18 top left, top right, 23, 27 inset & right, 52, 62 top left, 65, 139, 143, 150 bottom right, 158, 177 top, 194, 210; Steve Cole: 73, 82 top left; Amanda Clement: 92; Don Farrall: 98; C. Squared Studios: 110; Russell Illig: 111; S. Meltzer/Photolink: 210 top left; SW Productions: 210; Spike Mafford: 217 PHOTOFEST: 97, 116 THE STOCK MARKET: 137, 142, 156, 168; Mark Gamba: 76; Mug Shots: 99; Tom Stewart: 121; Chris Collins: 189; STONE: 65, 154, 160, 164, 176; Blake Little: 5, 9; Paul Rees: 7; Robert Daemmrich: 10; Dennis O'Clair: 12, 17 bottom left; Zigy Kaluzny: 15, 130; David Madison: 16; Steven Peters: 18 bottom right; Alan Levenson: 22; Ian Shaw: 24; Erik Butler: 25; Bob Thomas: 26; John Blaustein: 28; Lois & Bob Schlowsky: 31, 125; John & Eliza Forder: 37; John Lund: 38; Art Wolf: 47; Patrick Ingrand: 54; Darryl Torckler: 55; Ernest Braun: 56; Brad Hitz: 69; Doug Struthers: 73; Ian Shaw: 74; Jon Bradley: 80; Charles Gupton: 82 bottom left; Paul Chesley: 85; Daniel J. Cox: 99; David Woodfall: 99; Roger Tully: 99; Jeffrey Zaruba: 109; Mitch Kezar: 124; Jake Rajs: 129; Will & Deni Mcintyre: 131; Alan Klehr: 153; Doug Struthers: 167; Laurence Dutton: 193; Chris Thomaidis: 196; Ken Fisher: 198; Ed Honowitz: 198; Andrew Olney: 223; SUPERSTOCK: 177, 182, 185, 187, 188, 197, 212, 213, 221 bottom left THE STOCK MARKET: 5; 14; TIME WARNER TRADE PUBLISHING: 133: Phillip Hoose THE UNIVERSITY OF ARIZONA MUSEUM OF ART: Red CaNNA by Georgia O'Keeffe: 71

Illustrators:

Dlrk Wunderlich: Cover; Dave Jonason: 8, 18, 40, 90, 96, 114; Functional Art: Diane Ali, Batelman Illustration, Moffit Cecil, Adam Gordon, Larry Lee, John Quinn, Sintora Regina Vanderhorst, Michael Woo

Contents

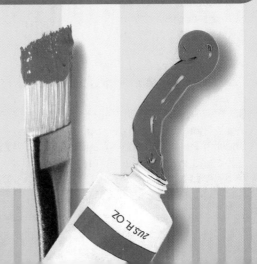

Opening the Olympics

Cheers explode from the excited crowd. The Olympic torch has entered the packed stadium. The proud runner holds the torch high. She runs past teams of athletes on the field. The opening ceremony has begun.

The Olympic flag waves. It has five linked rings on a white background. The rings stand for the friendship of people in the world's five major regions: Africa, the Americas, Asia, Australia, and Europe. The rings are blue, yellow, black, green, and red. Each country's flag has at least one of these colors.

Thousands of athletes stand with their teams. Their national flags flap in the breeze. The runner glides by, carrying the torch. Its flame was lit in Olympia, Greece. That is where the Olympics were first held nearly three thousand years ago. Now that is where the flame begins its journey each Olympic year.

When the runner lights the great Olympic flame, there is another loud roar. For the next two weeks, athletes from nearly two hundred countries will challenge each other's strength, speed, and skill. They will compete in the name of peace, good will, and understanding.

Let the Games begin!

Critical Thinking

1. **How are the Olympic Games different from other sports events?**

2. **What might athletes learn at the Olympic Games?**

3. **Do you think the Olympic Games are important? Explain.**

Word Study at Home

Visit us at www.sadlier-oxford.com

UNIT 1
Athletes

Opening the Olympics

Cheers explode from the excited crowd. The Olympic torch has entered the packed stadium. The proud runner holds the torch high. She runs past teams of athletes on the field. The opening ceremony has begun.

The Olympic flag waves. It has five linked rings on a white background. The rings stand for the friendship of people in the world's five major regions: Africa, the Americas, Asia, Australia, and Europe. The rings are blue, yellow, black, green, and red. Each country's flag has at least one of these colors.

Thousands of athletes stand with their teams. Their national flags flap in the breeze. The runner glides by, carrying the torch. Its flame was lit in Olympia, Greece. That is where the Olympics were first held nearly three thousand years ago. Now that is where the flame begins its journey each Olympic year.

When the runner lights the great Olympic flame, there is another loud roar. For the next two weeks, athletes from nearly two hundred countries will challenge each other's strength, speed, and skill. They will compete in the name of peace, good will, and understanding.

Let the Games begin!

Critical Thinking
1. How are the Olympic Games different from other sports events?
2. What might athletes learn at the Olympic Games?
3. Do you think the Olympic Games are important? Explain.

LESSON 1: Introduction to Consonant Blends and Consonant Digraphs   5

Dear Family,

Welcome to Sadlier's *Word Study* program. Each unit presents strategies and exercises to help your child become a better reader. In Unit 1, your child will review the different sounds of **c, g,** and **s** and will explore consonant blends and consonant digraphs. The theme of this unit is *athletes*.

A **consonant blend** is two or three consonants sounded together so that each letter is heard (**sp**eed, **spl**atter, ju**mp**er). Notice that the word **blend** begins and ends with a consonant blend!

A **consonant digraph** is two consonants that together stand for one sound (**ch**air, a**th**lete, ru**sh**). The word digra**ph** ends with the digraph **ph,** which makes the sound of **f.**

Family Focus

- Read together the passage on page 5 or an article from the sports page of your local newspaper. Discuss the article with your child. Have your child circle words with consonant blends and consonant digraphs. Offer your support by going over the work.

- Talk about sports or Olympic events that your family enjoys watching. Make a list of these events. Have each family member discuss his or her favorite. Ask what he or she likes most about the sport. Is it the players, the excitement, the competition—or all three?

LINKS TO LEARNING

To extend learning together, you might explore:

Web Sites
www.olympic-usa.org
www.devlab.dartmouth.edu/ olympic/history

Video
Atlanta's Olympic Glory, PBS Home Video.

Literature
100 Unforgettable Moments in the Summer Olympics by Robert Italia, ©1996.

Hour of the Olympics by Mary P. Osborne, ©1998.

Name _____

> **Helpful Hint**

The letter **c** usually has a soft sound when it is followed by **e, i,** or **y.** Otherwise, **c** has a hard sound.

poli**c**e **c**elery **c**ity la**c**y **c**able **c**omma **c**ute

★ Say each word in the box below.
Does it have a soft **c** or a hard **c**?

announce	basic	canoe	center	cereal	career
record	decide	local	score	spicy	voice

1. Write the soft **c** words on the lines below.

_____ _____ _____

_____ _____ _____

2. Write the hard **c** words on the lines below.

_____ _____ _____

_____ _____ _____

★ Complete each sentence with a word from the box above.

3. They'll _____ the players over the loudspeaker.

4. The _____ idea of the game is to earn points.

5. The coach will _____ on the batting order.

6. Our _____ park has a swimming pool.

7. I want to learn how to paddle a _____.

8. That player broke the home-run _____.

9. What was the final _____ of the game?

10. Did Jason lose his _____ cheering for the team?

> **CHALLENGE**

Each of the words below has a hard **c** *and* a soft **c** sound. Circle the soft **c.** Color the hard **c.**

bicycle
calcium
concert
currency

Helpful Hint

The letter **g** usually has a soft sound when it is followed by **e, i, or y.** The letters **dge** also have a soft **g** sound. Otherwise, **g** has a hard sound.

pigeon   magic   gym   nudge   game   golf   jog

⭐ **Say each word in the box. Does it have a soft g or a hard g?**

brag   cougar   energy   engine   gape   gentle

genius   fudge   goggles   gutter   goal   judge

1. Write the soft g words in the gym bag.

2. Write the hard g words in the golf bag.

⭐ **Complete each sentence with a word from the box above.**

3. A winner may _____ about an exciting game.

4. Roger Maris was a _____ with a baseball bat.

5. The batter stopped to _____ at his long home run.

6. In bowling, a _____ ball rolls off the lane.

7. A referee acts as a _____ in a sports event.

8. Long-distance runners need a lot of _____.

9. A racing car has a powerful _____.

10. Swimmers wear _____ to protect their eyes.

Home Involvement Activity Cut out pictures from a magazine of objects that have the hard g or soft g sound. Make two posters. Glue pictures with hard g words on one poster and pictures with soft g words on the other.

Name _____

> **Helpful Hint**
>
> **S** can stand for more than one sound.
>
> **s**alad   de**s**ert   **s**ugar

⭐ **Name each picture. Listen for three different sounds of s. Write the picture name on the line.**

1	2	3
_____	_____	_____

⭐ **Read the sentences. Circle each word that has the letter s. Then sort the circled words by the s sound. Write each word in the correct column.**

4. Real wrestling can be a school or an Olympic activity.

5. The sport surely takes a lot of practice.

6. Judges make sure that all matches are fair.

7. To win, you press the other person down onto the mat.

8. Once a player is pinned, the match ends.

> **CHALLENGE**
>
> Each word below has the sound of s in the middle. Say each word. Is the s like the s in **s**alad, de**s**ert, or **s**ugar?
>
> ti**ss**ue
> me**ss**age
> rea**s**on

s as in	s as in	s as in

⭐ **Complete each sentence with a word from the box. Use the sound clues to help you. Write a word only once.**

> soak   Use   bruise   sure   exercise   advise
>
> massage   muscle   physical   problems   Surely

1. Has too much _____ left you feeling sore?
   (s as in no**s**e)

2. Athletes often have minor _____ that need some kind of help.
   (s as in no**s**e)

3. After a hard game, they may have _____ aches.
   (s as in **s**ock)

4. Some athletes may find an ugly purple _____.
   (s as in no**s**e)

5. Experts in sports medicine _____ us to apply common sense.
   (s as in no**s**e)

6. A simple cure may be just a gentle _____.
   (s as in **s**ock)

7. A long _____ in a warm bath can also bring comfort.
   (s as in **s**ock)

8. _____ an ice pack to keep the swelling down.
   (s as in no**s**e)

9. More serious injuries may call for _____ therapy.
   (s as in no**s**e)

10. Be _____ to have a sports doctor judge what is best for you.
   (s as in **s**ugar)

11. _____, a visit to the doctor is worth the trouble.
   (s as in **s**ugar)

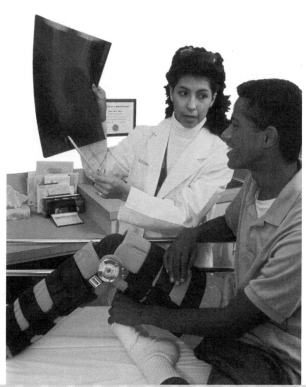

Home Involvement Activity Say aloud the names of family members, friends, teachers, pets, local streets, and other names that you know. Identify the kinds of s sounds you hear.

Name _____

Helpful Hint

A **consonant blend** is two or three consonants sounded together so that each letter is heard. An **initial consonant blend** appears at the beginning of a word.

blue   clerk   flood   glitter   plum   sled   twice

★ **Fill in the circle of the blend that begins each picture name. Then write the l-blend or the tw-blend on the line to complete the word.**

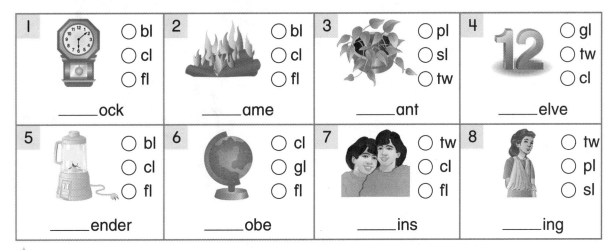

1	○ bl ○ cl ○ fl
	_____ock

2	○ bl ○ cl ○ fl
	_____ame

3	○ pl ○ sl ○ tw
	_____ant

4	○ gl ○ tw ○ cl
	_____elve

5	○ bl ○ cl ○ fl
	_____ender

6	○ cl ○ gl ○ fl
	_____obe

7	○ tw ○ cl ○ fl
	_____ins

8	○ tw ○ pl ○ sl
	_____ing

★ **Complete each sentence with the correct word below it. Write that word on the line.**

9. A _____ is a very small branch.
   tweet   twine   twig

10. Look up to see a puffy _____.
    clown   cloud   floor

11. The amusement park has a new water _____.
    slide   clue   glue

12. I left my baseball _____ at home.
    glove   bloom   plug

13. Vanilla is my favorite _____.
    flashlight   flavor   globe

CHALLENGE

Some city names begin with l-blends:

Bloomington
Flagstaff
Glendale
Plainview
Slippery Rock

List some others.

A **phonogram** is a syllable that has a vowel and any letters that follow. Usually, a phonogram has a vowel followed by one or more consonants. Here are some phonograms:

ace   ack   ay   eam   ide   ing   irl   ist   ock

★ **Each box has four initial l-blends and four phonograms. Match the blends and the phonograms to form words. Write the words on the lines.**

1			2		
bl	ay		cl	ace
pl	eam		gl	irl
tw	ack		tw	ock
gl	ist		pl	ide

_____

_____

_____

_____

★ **Choose the best word from the two boxes above to complete each sentence. Write the word on the line.**

3. High jumpers can _____ their bodies like pretzels to jump over the bar.

4. That baseball team can really _____ ball.

5. The karate champion has a _____ belt.

6. Ice skaters _____ across the ice.

7. Some ice skaters can spin or _____ so fast that you can barely see their eyes.

8. There were only two minutes left to play on the _____.

9. That basketball player has a _____ in his eye.

10. The winning team will _____ first in the league.

 Home Involvement Activity Make some l-blend cards to play a game. Mix the cards and place them face down. Take turns picking a card. Then say words that begin with the blend on the card. Play through the whole deck.

Name _____

Helpful Hint

Many consonants blend with r.
These words start with r-blends.

br**oom**   c**risp**   d**ragon**   f**rown**
g**ravel**   p**roject**   t**rack**

★ **Write an r-blend from the box below to complete each picture name.**

br	cr	dr	fr	gr	pr	tr

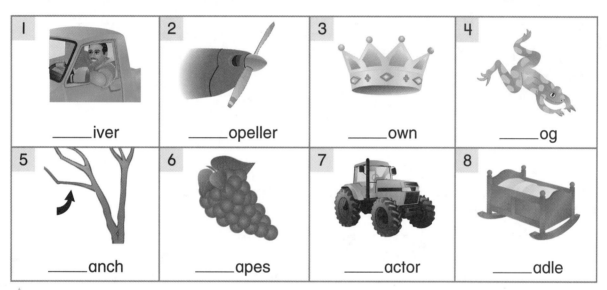

1 _____iver	2 _____opeller	3 _____own	4 _____og
5 _____anch	6 _____apes	7 _____actor	8 _____adle

★ **Complete each sentence with the correct word below it. Write that word on the line.**

9. A true _____ is on your side.
    trust   pride   friend

10. In math, we made a picture _____.
    graph   crown   trunk

11. Let's practice what to do in a fire _____.
    grill   drill   dream

12. How fast she goes around the _____!
    brain   track   drain

WORK TOGETHER

More English words start with s than with any other letter. With a partner, list as many s-blend words as you can to describe your school or class.

LESSON 5: **r-blends** and **s-blends**   **13**

Many consonants blend with **s**. These words start with **s**-blends.

scan   ski   slant   smart   sport   sting   swan

⭐ **Each word in the box starts with an s-blend. On the line, write the word from the box that names each picture.**

sponge   slide   smoke   skate   stadium   swimmer   snow   scale

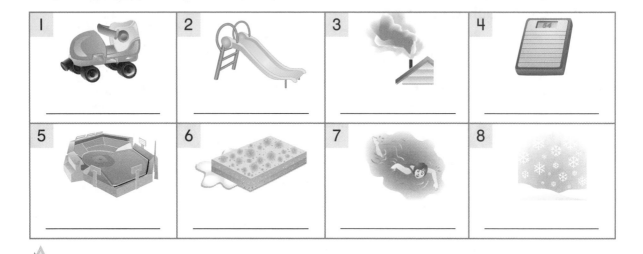

1	2	3	4
_____	_____	_____	_____

5	6	7	8
_____	_____	_____	_____

⭐ **Match the s-blends and the phonograms to form words. Write the words on the lines.**

9			10		
st		ip	st		in
sk		udge	sp		eet
sm		ick	sw		ilts
	_____			_____	
	_____			_____	
	_____			_____	

⭐ **Write a word from the two boxes above to complete the two *What if?* questions.**

11. What if a _____ left no stain?

12. What if lemons were _____?

LESSON 5: **r**-blends and **s**-blends

🏠 **Home Involvement Activity** Write *What if?* questions. Talk about how things would change if the *What if?* came true.

Name _____

> **Helpful Hint**

A **final consonant blend** appears at the end of a word.

fe**lt**   pi**nk**   la**mp**   wa**sp**   be**nd**   du**st**   ma**sk**

★ **Fill in the circle of the blend that ends each picture name. Then write the blend on the line to complete the word.**

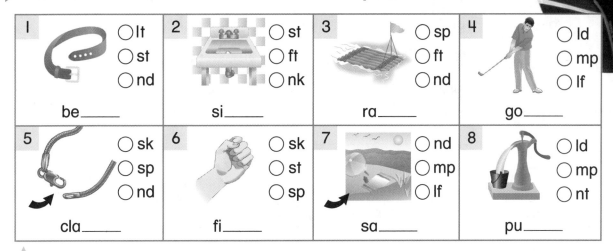

1	○ lt ○ st ○ nd	2	○ st ○ ft ○ nk	3	○ sp ○ ft ○ nd	4	○ ld ○ mp ○ lf
	be_____		si_____		ra_____		go_____
5	○ sk ○ sp ○ nd	6	○ sk ○ st ○ sp	7	○ nd ○ mp ○ lf	8	○ ld ○ mp ○ nt
	cla_____		fi_____		sa_____		pu_____

★ **Which word in each pair has a final consonant blend? Circle the word.**

9 While or wild	10 Grape or grasp	11 Gold or goal	12 tent or ten
13 Bunt or but	14 Blare or blast	15 Take or task	16 Wool or wolf

★ **Write a word from the box to complete each sentence.**

> fault   shield   wound

17. Athletes wear special gear to _____ them from getting hurt.

18. Sports accidents can happen, yet no one is

    at _____.

19. Being hit by a hockey puck can _____ you.

> **WORK TOGETHER**
>
> Form a small group. One person says a word with a final blend, such as **col**d. The next person says a word with a final blend that begins with the last letter of **col**d, such as **d**us**t**. Keep a word list.

A **syllable** is any of the parts into which a word may be divided at the end of a line. Many words with **consonant blends** have more than one syllable.

play-er   pri-va-cy   snow-board

⭐ Say each word in the box. Sort the words by how many syllables they have. Write each word in the correct column.

grasp	drama	sneaker	sport	statistics
dart	creative	flag	president	platform
mound	probably	request	trainer	uniform

1

One Syllable

_____
_____
_____
_____

2

Two Syllables

_____
_____
_____
_____

3

Three Syllables

_____
_____
_____
_____

⭐ **Each team below has one consonant blend. Circle each one-syllable name. Draw one line under each two-syllable name. Draw two lines under the three-syllable names.**

4. Clippers   5. Blues   6. Sliders

7. Predators   8. Stingrays   9. Twins

10. Colts   11. Dragons   12. Yellowhawks

LESSON 6: Final Blends and
Syllables with Blends

 Home Involvement Activity Work together to list words that rhyme with these words: **bend, camp, tent, gold, mist, pink, task.** Try to find at least two rhymes for each word.

Name _____

⭐ **Read about a new Olympic sport.
Then answer the questions that follow.**

Beach Volleyball

by Martin Lee and Marcia Miller

At the 1992 Summer Olympics, a new event was introduced. Fans flocked to see the exciting game of beach volleyball. Beach volleyball is—you got it—volleyball played outdoors on sand.

Beach volleyball began on the beaches of California about 75 years ago. Yet the first tournament wasn't held until 1948. The winners got a case of soda. Now the game is a professional sport. Today's winners get big prize money. In the 1996 Olympics, 24 men's teams and 16 women's teams played for their countries. The U.S. men's and women's teams won gold medals.

The rules for playing beach volleyball are much like those for playing the indoor game. The court is about the same size. It is a flat rectangle 59 feet long and 29 1/2 feet wide. The big difference is in the surface. The sand for beach volleyball must be at least 12 inches deep.

Beach volleyball teams may have two, three, four, or six players. Unlike indoor players, beach volleyball team members can wear clothing with different colors and designs. They can wear sunglasses, hats, or visors. They can even play barefoot.

Beach volleyball takes a lot of energy. Yet players can tumble without getting scraped. Sand softens every fall. If you enjoy playing in the sun, beach volleyball may be your sport.

 Reader's Response

1. **How is beach volleyball like volleyball played indoors?**

2. **How are the two games different?**

3. **Which type of volleyball would you rather play? Why?**

LESSON 7: Connecting Reading and Writing Comprehension—Compare and Contrast; Synthesize

Every sport has its rules. Choose a sport or a game that you enjoy. What is the object of the game? Think about its rules. For example, how many players are needed? What does each player do? How does the game begin? How do you keep score?

Make a list of rules for playing the sport you choose. Use at least two of these words to help you write your list of rules.

block	contest	first	second	last	point
swing	protect	score	sport	twice	triumph

Writer's Tips

Jot down the name of the sport at the top of your list. Write the rules in an order that makes sense.

Writer's Challenge

Use the sport you wrote about or another sport you like. Imagine playing it in a totally different way. For example, how would you play soccer on ice? How would you play softball with a beach ball? Write a list of rules for this new game. Have fun!

Name _____

⭐ **Name each picture below. Fill in the circle of the letter or letters that complete the picture name. Then write the letter or letters on the line.**

1	○ c ○ k ○ cl	2	○ tw ○ gr ○ gl	3	○ s ○ c ○ g
_____anoe		_____ove		_____elery	

4	○ g ○ s ○ kl	5	○ tr ○ gr ○ dr	6	○ sw ○ tw ○ sl
_____oggles		_____iver		_____immer	

7	○ sk ○ sl ○ sp	8	○ g ○ gu ○ c	9	○ c ○ s ○ z
_____ate		pi_____eon		_____ougar	

10	○ dr ○ fr ○ pr	11	○ z ○ c ○ s	12	○ sl ○ fr ○ sp
_____og		de_____ert		_____ed	

⭐ **Write the word from the box below that answers each question.**

> celery   race   skull   sneaker   twelve   wolf

13. Which is a fierce animal? _____

14. Which is a vegetable? _____

15. Which is a contest of speed? _____

16. Which is a kind of athletic shoe? _____

17. Which protects your brain? _____

18. Which number comes after eleven? _____

Fill in the circle of the word that completes each sentence. Then write the word on the line.

1. People who like to fish enjoy the _____ of waiting.
   ○ trance   ○ pleasure   ○ price

2. They can _____ hours waiting for a fish to bite.
   ○ blend   ○ train   ○ spend

3. Yet fishing is not just a warm weather _____.
   ○ spirit   ○ sport   ○ sponge

4. Even on frozen lakes, some people have a _____ way to fish.
   ○ clever   ○ craft   ○ cleaner

5. They use tools to _____ holes in the solid ice covering the water.
   ○ twirl   ○ grill   ○ drill

6. They _____ fishing lines down the holes into the cold water.
   ○ drop   ○ draw   ○ drip

7. Ice fishing calls for _____ patience.
   ○ gravy   ○ green   ○ great

8. It also requires ice fishers to _____ warmly.
   ○ dress   ○ dream   ○ press

9. Some ice fishers build _____ huts over their fishing holes.
   ○ spell   ○ small   ○ still

10. This allows them to _____ warm and dry.
   ○ stand   ○ sway   ○ stay

Extend & Apply

Think of a sports word that fits each clue. Write the word on the line.

11. It begins with a blend. _____
12. It has an s-blend. _____
13. It has a hard g sound. _____
14. It has one syllable. _____
15. It ends with a blend. _____
16. It has an r-blend. _____
17. It has a soft c sound. _____
18. It has two syllables. _____

Name _____

Helpful Hint

A **consonant digraph** is two consonants that together stand for one sound. **Initial digraphs** begin words. **Final digraphs** end words.

| Initial digraphs: | channel | shape | thunder | whale |
| Final digraphs: | blush | math | peach | pluck |

★ **Say** the first word in each row. Listen for the initial consonant digraph. Then circle two pictures in the row that have the same consonant digraph in their names. Write all the words on the lines.

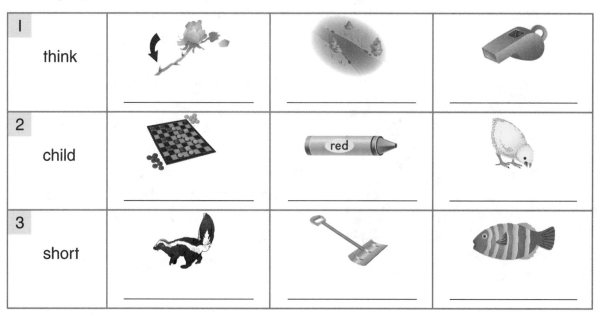

1 think			
2 child			
3 short			

★ **Fill** in the circle of the word that completes each sentence. Then write the word on the line.

4. Let's hang the team banner from the highest

_____
○ branch   ○ starch   ○ gulch

5. The team will _____ onto the field.
○ flesh   ○ rush   ○ mush

6. We were happy to win the _____ game.
○ charge   ○ third   ○ whale

CHALLENGE

Each word below begins with a digraph:

chin

shoulder

thumb

List three other words for each initial digraph above.

Helpful Hint

The digraph **ch** can make three different sounds. Usually, it makes the sound you hear at the start of **ch**ain or at the end of **lun**ch. Yet sometimes, it makes the sound of **sh**, as in **ch**ute, or the sound of **k**, as in **ch**emical.

Read the paragraph. Underline each word that has the digraph ch. Then sort the underlined words by the ch sound they make. Write each word in the correct column below.

Mrs. Chevron is our team trainer. She also runs the school pep club. The pep club gets fans to cheer at the games. "We don't need help making noise," some people say. Yet our trainer won't take such excuses. "Noise inspires a team," she always says.

At the last game, our team trainer wore a scarf of red chiffon. She waved it in the air to charge up the crowd. Then she led us in a chorus of the "Chicago Chant." Those loud musical chords must have worked! It was pure chaos when Chris made the winning goal. Afterward, the teacher treated the team and the pep club to hot chocolate. Yum!

1 Ch as in chain	2 Ch as in chute	3 Ch as in chemical

Home Involvement Activity Make two lists of sports words. In the first list, write three words with initial digraphs. List three words with final digraphs in the second list.

Name _____

Helpful Hint

Each of these words has a **consonant digraph** in the middle.

au**th**or   friend**sh**ip   some**wh**ere   ta**ck**le   wood**ch**uck

⭐ **Name each picture. Listen for the consonant digraph.**
Then write the digraph on the line to complete the word.

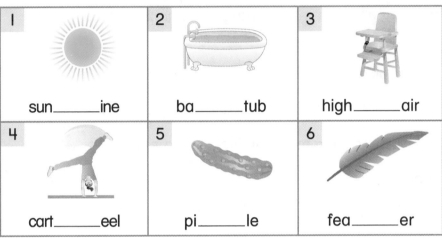

1 sun_____ine	2 ba_____tub	3 high_____air
4 cart_____eel	5 pi_____le	6 fea_____er

⭐ **Read the story. Fill in each blank with a word from the box.**
Then circle the consonant digraph in each word you write.

bashful   birthday   everywhere   anything   Together   tackled

Joshua found out the date of our teacher's **(7)** _____.
We decided to plan a surprise. Jackie made a card we

could all sign. **(8)** _____, we wrote a funny poem.

We wouldn't let **(9)** _____ spoil our fun.
The students chipped in to get the teacher a fancy notebook.

We **(10)** _____ the job of drawing a class picture.

We hung paper chains and balloons **(11)** _____.
Then we hid. When we heard our teacher's voice, we yelled,
"Surprise!" Our teacher was amazed. She looked almost

(12) _____!

CHALLENGE

Some words have more than one consonant digraph. Two examples are **chick**en and **wh**e**th**er. How many double digraph words can you think of? List them.

Each word in the box has the consonant digraph ph or gh. Write the word on the line that best completes each sentence.

| alphabet | dolphin | laugh | Phoenix | rough | triumph | trophy |

1. A funny joke can cause you to _____ out loud.

2. The winner of the contest will get a silver _____.

3. The _____ is a mammal that lives in the sea.

4. The opposite of *smooth* is _____.

5. Another word for *victory* or *success* is _____.

6. The _____ is another name for the ABCs.

7. The capital of Arizona is _____.

Say each word. Listen for the consonant digraph. Then sort the words according to where the consonant digraph appears in the word: at the beginning, in the middle, or at the end.

| bench | leather | theater | footpath | shovel | paragraph |
| physical | cashier | tickle | telephone | whimper | attach |

8 Initial Digraph	9 Medial Digraph	10 Final Digraph
_____	_____	_____
_____	_____	_____
_____	_____	_____
_____	_____	_____

LESSON 10: Medial Consonant Digraphs; ph and gh

 Home Involvement Activity Brainstorm a list of names of people that have consonant digraphs. The digraphs can be at the beginning, as in **Sh**aron, at the end, as in **Joseph**, or in the middle, as in **Ra**ch**el**.

Name _____

Helpful Hint

Some **consonant blends** are made up of three letters. You will find three-letter blends in words like **spl**inter, **scr**eam, and **thr**ob. Here are some three-letter consonant blends:

chr   sch   scr   shr   spl   spr   str   thr

⭐ **Write the word that completes each sentence.
Use one of the three-letter blends from the box.**

1. Dad's first car had _____ome fenders.

2. Baseball season starts again each _____ing.

3. It takes a _____ong swimmer to battle big waves.

4. Here is the _____edule for the chess tournament.

5. Hippos like to _____ash in the water.

6. The cage is made of metal _____eening.

7. There are _____ools to teach people how to drive.

8. Lemon drops can make your _____oat feel better.

9. The ball rolled into the thick _____ubs.

10. The king sits on a velvet _____one.

⭐ **Unscramble the letters to name the picture.
Then write the unscrambled name on the line.**

11 misprh	12 paserc	13 clohos
_____	_____	_____
14 hdtare	15 yaprs	16 warts
_____	_____	_____

CHALLENGE

You know that u is not a consonant. Yet **squ-** can be a three-letter consonant blend.

Circle the **squ-** blend in these words. Then list other words that have the **squ-** blend.

squash
squeal
squirm

Use a word from the box for each clue. Write one letter in each space. Read down the shaded column to answer the question. Hint: The answer below has a digraph in the middle.

| Christopher | dolphin | split | spread | scheme | screech |
| shredded | laughter | sprinkle | strength | thread | shrink |

1. a gentle, short rainfall   _ _ _ _ _ _ _ _

2. power or force   _ _ _ _ _ _ _ _

3. torn into narrow strips or pieces   _ _ _ _ _ _ _ _

4. a fancy bed cover   _ _ _ _ _ _

5. a friendly sea mammal   _ _ _ _ _ _ _

6. to separate into parts   _ _ _ _ _

7. a wild or crazy plan   _ _ _ _ _ _

8. a kind of owl that makes a loud noise   _ _ _ _ _ _ _

9. to get smaller   _ _ _ _ _ _

10. a sound that shows humor or joy   _ _ _ _ _ _ _ _

11. the first name of Mr. Columbus   _ _ _ _ _ _ _ _ _ _ _

12. very thin string for sewing   _ _ _ _ _ _

Question: In this race, horses jump over ditches, hedges, and hurdles. A form of this race is for humans, too. What is this race called?

Answer: _____

Name _____

Read each group of words. Say and spell each word in bold print. Repeat the word. Then sort the words according to where the digraph appears in the word. Write each word in the correct column below.

- play in the **sunshine**

- soccer **champion**

- **crouch** behind the plate

- **tackle** the player

- the **north** field

- by an unknown **athlete**

- our favorite **teacher**

- **rather** than wait

- **astonish** the fans

- cast a **shadow**

- a team **photo**

- won a **tough** game

- a silver **trophy**

- wait over **there**

- celebrate a **triumph**

- a **chorus** of smiles

Initial Consonant Digraph	Medial Consonant Digraph	Final Consonant Digraph

Many of today's athletes are modern-day heroes. These people are superstars on and off the field. Today, many sports figures are more than super athletes. They are also super people who help the people in their community.

Choose an athlete you admire. Write this athlete a letter. Give three strong reasons to explain why you admire him or her. Ask the athlete some questions. Use at least two of these spelling words in your letter.

| sunshine | champion | crouch | tackle | north | athlete | teacher | rather |
| astonish | shadow | photo | tough | trophy | there | triumph | chorus |

_____ [Your address]

_____

_____ [Date]

[Greeting] **Dear** _____,

[Body] _____

_____

_____

_____

_____

_____

_____

Sincerely, [Closing]

_____ [Signature]

Writer's Tip

Use letter parts correctly. Write your address, the date, and the name of your athlete. Include your reasons and questions in the body. Close with "Sincerely," and sign your name.

Speaker's Challenge

Imagine that you are a sportscaster on the local TV news. Give a description of a real or an imaginary game in which the athlete you wrote about was the star. Vary the tone of your voice to give facts and to stress the excitement of the game.

Name _____

Read each sentence. Listen for the sound that the underlined letters make. Then circle another word in the sentence that has the same sound.

1. <u>Ph</u>ysical education is my favorite subject.

2. The player should remove the ball from the <u>ch</u>ute.

3. She'd ra<u>th</u>er swim in shorts and a T-shirt than in a swimsuit.

4. Boxers need to be tou<u>gh</u> for many important reasons.

5. Our <u>sch</u>ool teams score many points.

6. How many TV sports <u>ch</u>annels will there be in the future?

7. <u>Ch</u>ris loves to celebrate a win by having chocolate ice cream.

8. Fans lau<u>gh</u> and cheer at the team mascot's silly tricks.

9. The <u>ch</u>ildren of today may be the new champs of tomorrow.

10. Today, many a<u>thl</u>etes enjoy wealth and fame.

Each of these people was a famous athlete. Circle the number of syllables in each person's last name.

11. Jackie Robinson   I   2   3

12. Walter Payton   I   2   3

13. Bobby Jones   I   2   3

14. Wilma Rudolph   I   2   3

15. Joe Louis   I   2   3

16. Arthur Ashe   I   2   3

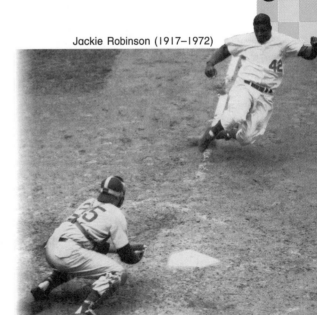

Jackie Robinson (1917–1972)

Read about a wonderful athlete. For each numbered blank, there is a choice of words below. Fill in the circle of the word that best completes the sentence.

Mildred Didrikson Zaharias was the **1** female athlete of her day. She was born in Texas in 1914 and was called "Babe." Babe won more **2** and set more records in more sports than any other athlete. This includes both women *and* men! She was the star of her high school basketball team. Babe also played on track-and-field teams in college. She played eight other sports, too. Babe even **3** a whole inning of a major league baseball game. Then she decided to play golf. Of course, she <u>had a knack for</u> that sport, too! As a golfer, she lost only one **4** in seven years! Babe died in 1956. Yet she was one of the best athletes of the twentieth century.

1. ○ greatest ○ closest ○ clearest ○ strictest

2. ○ benches ○ splits ○ trophies ○ scrapes

3. ○ graphed ○ roughed ○ blushed ○ pitched

4. ○ month ○ mesh ○ match ○ march

Read the passage again to answer these questions. Circle the letter of the answer.

5. What made Babe Didrikson Zaharias such a great athlete?

   a. She was born in Texas.

   b. She played basketball in high school.

   c. She starred in many different sports.

   d. She took part in a baseball game.

6. What does the phrase <u>had a knack for</u> mean?

   a. liked to collect things

   b. was good at

   c. tried to learn

   d. wanted to avoid

Extend & Apply

Suppose you could ask Babe Didrikson Zaharias a question. What would you want to know? Write your question here.

_____

What a Deal!

People have been exploring new places for centuries. North America is just one place that adventurers have explored.

Few American colonists lived west of the Appalachian Mountains before 1776. Yet some people did cross these mountains. One of these early explorers was Daniel Boone. Boone followed old Native American trails to a pass in the mountains. This pass was called the Cumberland Gap. From there, he led families west to settle on land in Kentucky.

Soon, the United States owned the land as far west as the Mississippi River. Yet the country needed more land for its many settlers. France owned all the land west of the Mississippi River. Would France sell some of this land?

The year was 1803. President Thomas Jefferson wanted to buy the port of New Orleans from France. To his surprise, France wanted to sell more than just New Orleans. "How much will you give for the whole of Louisiana?" a French official asked. Jefferson said just $15 million. France agreed to his price. For just four cents an acre, the President had doubled the size of the United States! This land deal is called the Louisiana Purchase. A year later, Lewis and Clark would begin to explore this land. Their journey would lead the way for the pioneers to go west—all the way to the Pacific Ocean.

Critical Thinking

1. Why did people want to go west?

2. What made the Louisiana Purchase such a "good deal"?

3. Would you have gone west with the pioneers? Why or why not?

LESSON 14: Introduction to Short and Long Vowels, **r**-controlled Vowels, Vowel Pairs, Vowel Digraphs, Diphthongs, and Phonograms

31

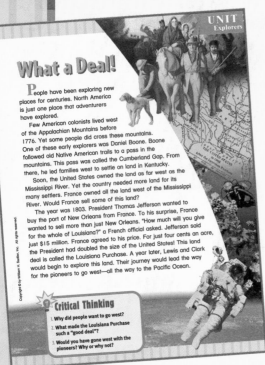

What a Deal!

People have been exploring new places for centuries. North America is just one place that adventurers have explored.

Few American colonists lived west of the Appalachian Mountains before 1776. Yet some people did cross these mountains. One of these early explorers was Daniel Boone. Boone followed old Native American trails to a pass in the mountains. This pass was called the Cumberland Gap. From there, he led families west to settle on land in Kentucky.

Soon, the United States owned the land as far west as the Mississippi River. Yet the country needed more land for its many settlers. France owned all the land west of the Mississippi River. Would France sell some of this land?

The year was 1803. President Thomas Jefferson wanted to buy the port of New Orleans from France. To his surprise, France wanted to sell more than just New Orleans. "How much will you give for the whole of Louisiana?" a French official asked. Jefferson said just $15 million. France agreed to his price. For just four cents an acre, the President had doubled the size of the United States! This land deal is called the Louisiana Purchase. A year later, Lewis and Clark would begin to explore this land. Their journey would lead the way for the pioneers to go west—all the way to the Pacific Ocean.

Critical Thinking

1. Why did people want to go west?
2. What made the Louisiana Purchase such a "good deal"?
3. Would you have gone west with the pioneers? Why or why not?

Dear Family,

Your child is about to begin Unit 2 of Sadlier's *Word Study* program. In this unit, students will examine short and long vowels as well as **r**-controlled vowels, vowel pairs, vowel digraphs, diphthongs, and phonograms. The theme of this unit is *explorers*.

A **vowel pair** is two vowels sounded together to make one long vowel sound. The first vowel in the pair has the long sound of its name, and the second vowel is silent (tr**ai**n, sn**ee**ze).

A **vowel digraph** is two vowels sounded together to make a long or short sound (p**ie**ce, sw**ea**ter), or a special sound (l**oo**k).

A **diphthong** is two vowels blended together as one sound (c**oi**n, b**oy**, cl**ou**d, cr**ow**n).

Family Focus

- Read together the passage on page 31. Discuss whether you and your family might have joined the pioneers who went west in the early 1800s. Then reread the passage. Have your child circle words with vowel pairs, vowel digraphs, and diphthongs.

- Look at the photographs of the scuba diver and the astronaut on page 31. How are these people explorers? Have your family brainstorm ideas to create a list of occupations that employ people who could be called the explorers of today.

LINKS TO LEARNING

To extend learning together, you might explore:

Web Sites
www.kidinfo.com/American_History/Explorers.html
www.nara.gov/exhall/originals/loupurch.html

Video
Lewis & Clark, a film by Ken Burns, PBS Home Video.

Literature
The Exploration of North America by Shirley Greenway, ©1998.

The Journals of Lewis and Clark: A New Selection, ©1964.

Name _____

Helpful Hints

If a word or syllable has only one vowel, either at the beginning of the word or syllable or between two consonants, the vowel usually has the **short** sound.

h**a**nd   s**e**ll   s**i**ck   f**i**n   h**o**p   b**u**mp

Note: The words above contain phonograms.
A **phonogram** is a syllable that has a vowel and any letters that follow. Look at these phonograms:

and   **ell**   **ick**   **in**   **op**   **ump**

Read each picture name. Underline the words in the row that have the same phonogram as the name of the picture.

1. **pin** 🔗   spin   chip   plan   tin   grin   pen   fin

2. **bell** 🔔   fell   ball   sell   stall   tell   swell   bend

3. **stump** 🪵   dump   damp   lump   bump   bum   stamp   drum

4. **stand** 🎼   land   ramp   sand   hand   band   sing   and

Helpful Hint

Y can stand for **short** i, **long** i, and **long** e.

short i: s**y**stem   **long** i: fl**y**   **long** e: stor**y**

Say the words in the box below. Then sort the words.

| dry | penny | gym |

5 Short i sound	6 Long i sound	7 Long e sound

WORK TOGETHER

Use phonograms to write a short poem about exploring. Have a partner circle the phonograms you use.

If there are two vowels in a one-syllable word, the first vowel is usually **long,** and the second vowel is silent.

heat   coat   kite   snake   stone

If a word or syllable has one vowel and that vowel comes at the end of the word or syllable, the vowel usually has the **long** sound.

me   go   staple   puny   cider

Aztec-Puebla mask

⭐ **Read each word. Write S if the vowel or vowels in red have a short sound. Write L if the vowel or vowels in red have a long sound.**

1. he___   2. plane ___   3. pupil ___   4. moat ___   5. pony ___

6. legal___   7. piper ___   8. meat ___   9. stable ___   10. wait ___

⭐ **Underline each word that has the same phonogram as the word at the top of the list.**

11. **pray**	12. **rice**	13. **sing**	14. **pick**	15. **neat**
stay	price	sang	sick	creep
spray	glide	ring	pack	seat
plane	race	pill	pluck	heat
hay	twice	wing	click	beat

⭐ **Read each sentence. Underline the word with the same vowel sound as the word in bold print.**

16. Explorers crossed the seas in ships made from **trees**.

17. Some people **set** out looking for goods to sell and to trade.

18. Explorers brought slaves all the **way** from West Africa.

19. For other explorers, the plan was to try to **find** land for their countries.

20. As a **rule**, sailors stayed cool by resting below deck.

21. Some of these sailors were **bold** and boastful.

22. After many months at sea, most sailors were glad to be **home** again.

23. Those who **stayed** at sea faced many hardships.

LESSON 15: Short and Long Vowels; y as a Vowel

🏠 **Home Involvement Activity** List the titles of favorite books, movies, songs, magazines, or TV shows. Circle each short vowel sound. Underline each long vowel sound.

Name _____

Helpful Hint

When an r follows a vowel, the vowel has a new sound.
The letters ar have the vowel sound you hear in art.
The letters or have the vowel sound you hear in horse.

arm   guitar   park   porch   sport   form

★ Write the letters ar or or to complete the name of
   each picture.

| 1 sh____k | 2 t____ch | 3 h____n | 4 c____d |
| 5 d____t | 6 f____m | 7 h____p | 8 f____t |

Hernando
Cortés
(1485–1547)

★ The box below has four phonograms. Use each phonogram
   once to complete the words in the sentences.

| ake | ame | ip | ore |

9. In the 1500s, Spanish explorers would t_____
   soldiers to North America.

10. They made this tr_____ in the hope of finding gold.

11. Coronado was a Spanish explorer who came to find

    riches and f_____.

12. Hernando Cortés would also expl_____ North
    America in the hope of finding silver and gold.

CHALLENGE

Ar**mor** starts with
the r-controlled
vowel ar. List as
many other words
that start with ar
as you can. Here
are two examples:

arm

art

Look at these different spellings for the same vowel sound.

wh**ir**l   f**er**n   bl**ur**b   w**or**ld

Notice that **or** can stand for this sound, too.

Map of the World: *The Americas*, c 1579

⭐ **Underline the word that names each picture. Then write the word on the line.**

1	crib curb curl	2	shirt short chart	3	garble germ gerbil
4	title turtle turn	**5**	worm warm word	**6**	head herd hurt

⭐ **Underline the word that completes each sentence. Then write the word on the line**

7. There is a _____ on the window sill.
   turn   world   bird

8. We had to _____ to miss the oncoming car.
   serve   hurt   swerve

9. Our soccer team finished _____ in the league.
   third   whirling   dirty

10. My great-grandmother used to _____ her own butter.
    smirk   whirl   churn

11. My mother seemed to carry everything she owned in her _____.
    twirl   perch   purse

12. Will you be able to _____ on the poster tomorrow?
    squirm   work   curve

LESSON 16: r-controlled Vowels **ar, er, ir, or, ur**

 Home Involvement Activity Have a phonics **scaveng**er hunt! W**or**k together to look for things around your home that have names with **r**-controlled vowels. List all the words that you find. Try f**or** at least ten words.

Name _____

> **Helpful Hint**

Here are three different spellings for the same vowel sound.

st**air**　　　　sp**are**　　　　sw**ear**

★ **Say** the picture in each box. Then combine the phonogram with the letter or letters to build words that have the same vowel sound.

1	2	3
air	**are**	**ear**
p_____	fl_____	b_____
f_____	sp_____	p_____
ch_____	sh_____	w_____
st_____	gl_____	sw_____

Cave explorer

★ **Fill in the circle of the word that completes each sentence. Then write the word on the line.**

4. What should you _____ to explore a cave?
   ○ wear　　○ blare　　○ dare

5. Some explorers _____ to go where no one has gone before.
   ○ flare　　○ dare　　○ share

6. Would it _____ you to take a trip into space?
   ○ tear　　○ clear　　○ scare

7. The captain of the ship was _____ to the crew.
   ○ rare　　○ aware　　○ fair

8. The divers saw _____ sea creatures below.
   ○ rare　　○ hair　　○ air

> **CHALLENGE**

What do you notice about the words **b**are and **b**ear? About **h**are and **h**air? Use each pair of words in a sentence.

The letters **ear** and **eer** can stand for the same vowel sound.

y**ear**   cl**ear**   d**eer**   sn**eer**

Ear can also stand for the sound you hear in **ear**l.

⭐ **Say the picture in each box. Then combine the phonogram with the letter or letters to build words that have the same vowel sound.**

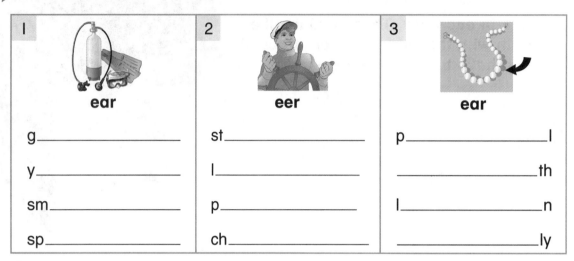

1	2	3
ear	**eer**	**ear**
g_____	st_____	p_____l
y_____	l_____	_____th
sm_____	p_____	l_____n
sp_____	ch_____	_____ly

⭐ **Complete each sentence with a word from the boxes above.**

4. The divers found a _____ in that oyster shell.

5. The captain found it hard to _____ the ship.

6. We put on our scuba _____ and dove into the water.

7. We got an _____ start in order to reach shore before nightfall.

8. Sailors used to _____ mud on themselves to protect their skin from the sun.

9. The captain can _____ through his spyglass.

10. When we reached dry land, we let out a loud _____.

11. People have explored nearly every corner of the _____.

12. Last _____, the shuttle explored outer space.

LESSON 17: **r**-controlled Vowels
air, are, ear, eer

Home Involvement Activity Make word webs for the **r**-controlled vowel sounds **air, are, ear,** and **eer.** List as many words for each sound as you can.

⭐ **Read about the journey of the explorers Lewis and Clark. Then answer the questions that follow.**

The Journey of Lewis and Clark

Now that the United States had made the Louisiana Purchase, President Thomas Jefferson wanted to know more about the land. What did it look like? Who lived on it? What plants grew there? What animals made it their home? To get answers, Jefferson sent his friend Meriwether Lewis to explore the Louisiana Purchase.

In 1804, Lewis and his friend William Clark began their trip through the West. They had about forty men with them. The group left from St. Louis and sailed up the Missouri River. The explorers got help from the people they met. For example, they met Sacajawea (sah kah jah WEE uh), a young Shoshone woman. She spoke to the Shoshone and to other groups for them. She also guided the explorers part of the way. Her brother, a Shoshone chief, gave the group horses for crossing the Rocky Mountains. From there, the explorers would follow the Columbia River to the Pacific Ocean. Along the way, Lewis mapped all the routes.

The journey of Lewis and Clark was not easy. Yet, Lewis and Clark wrote down in their journals all that they saw. Today, you can still read what they wrote. You can also see what they saw by following the Lewis and Clark Trail.

Sacajawea Leading Lewis and Clark
by Alfred Russell

Reader's Response

1. Why did Thomas Jefferson want Lewis to explore the Louisiana Purchase?

2. What kinds of problems did Lewis and Clark face on their journey? How do you think they solved them?

3. Would you like to follow the Lewis and Clark Trail? Give three reasons.

LESSON 18: Connecting Reading and Writing Comprehension—Problem and Solution; Synthesize

39

READ & WRITE

Like Lewis and Clark, many explorers have described their travels in a journal. Good descriptions in a journal help a writer to remember an experience. They also help readers to picture what the writer has seen and felt on the trip.

Now it's your turn to write in a travel journal. Describe a trip you have taken. Write an entry for a day in which you solved a problem on the trip. Include strong details. Use at least two of these words in your journal entry.

careful	dare	share	plane	peer	boat
world	trip	explore	car	problem	solve

Date: _____

Place: _____

Problem: _____

_____

_____

Solution: _____

_____

_____

_____

_____

Writer's Tip

Use vivid verbs and vivid adjectives in your details to let your readers see and feel what you saw, did, and felt.

Writer's Challenge

Imagine that you are Meriwether Lewis or William Clark. Write a journal entry for a day on which you solved a difficult problem. Use vivid details to describe the experience.

Name _____

Helpful Hint

A **vowel pair** is two vowels sounded together to make one long vowel sound. The first vowel in the pair has the long sound of its name, and the second vowel is silent. The vowel pairs **ai** and **ay** have the **long a** sound. Listen:

We visited **Spain** tod**ay**.   The **rain** began **yesterday**.

⭐ **Write the letters ai or ay to complete the name of each picture.**

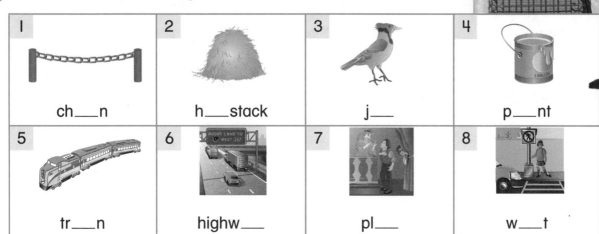

1	2	3	4
ch___n	h___stack	j___	p___nt

5	6	7	8
tr___n	highw___	pl___	w___t

Statue of
Don Quixote
de la Mancha

⭐ **Add one or more consonants before each phonogram. Be sure the words fit the clues.**

9. a country in Europe _____ain

10. another word for *mind* _____ain

11. something used to catch fish _____ait

12. a surprise attack _____aid

13. the month before June _____ay

14. to express in words _____ay

16. a small body of water _____ay

17. the opposite of sad _____ay

CHALLENGE

A line from the musical *My Fair Lady* says, "The **rain** in **Spain** st**ay**s **mainly** in the **plain**." Make up 3 other sentences with words that repeat the vowel pairs **ai** and **ay**.

LESSON 19: Vowel Pairs **ai, ay, ee, ea** and Vowel Digraph **ea**

41

The **vowel pair** ee always has the long e sound.

Bee**s** make me **sn**ee**ze!**

The **vowel pair** ea also has the **long** e sound, as in **s**ea**t.** When ea has the **short** e sound, it is a **vowel digraph.**

I left my **sw**ea**ter** on the bus.

Say each word in the box. Then sort the words. Write each word in the correct column in the chart.

| feather | referee | jeans | measure | agree | eagle | seen | heed |
| bean | spread | cheese | thread | flea | easel | meadow | |

1 ea **as short** e	2 ea **as long** e	3 ee **as long** e
_____	_____	_____
_____	_____	_____
_____	_____	_____
_____	_____	_____
_____	_____	_____

Complete each sentence. Use the words from the chart above.

4. The _____ called a foul on the basketball player.

5. The cows were asleep in the _____.

6. The tiny _____ can't fly, but it can jump!

7. Is it hard for you to _____ a needle?

8. The painter worked at an _____.

9. A graceful _____ soared above us.

10. I saved a _____ from the bird.

LESSON 19: Vowel Pairs **ai, ay, ee,**
ea and Vowel Digraph **ea**

Home Involvement Activity The words **read** and **read** have two different meanings and are pronounced differently. Use both words in a sentence that makes sense. Then do the same for **lead** and **lead.**

Name _____

Helpful Hints

The **vowel pair** ei has the **long** e sound. Listen:

receive   seize   leisure

The **vowel digraphs** ei and ey can have the **long** a sound.

sleigh   they   obey

Note: A **vowel digraph** can have a long or short sound. Like a vowel pair, a vowel digraph is two vowels sounded together to make one sound.

⭐ **Say each word in the box. Then sort the words. Write each word in the correct column in the chart.**

| sleigh | convey | reins | seize | neither | deceive |
| obey | eight | either | survey | weight | they |

1 ei **as in** rec**ei**ved	2 ei **as in** n**ei**ghbor	3 ey **as in** pr**ey**
_____	_____	_____
_____	_____	_____
_____	_____	_____
_____	_____	_____

⭐ **Underline the words in each sentence that have the same vowel sound as the sound at the beginning of the row.**

4. **Long** a   They say that wolves prey on reindeer.

5. **Long** a   My eight neighbors receive mail.

6. **Long** e   Please seize the reins of the sleigh.

CHALLENGE

The letters ey can also make the **long** e sound, as in **key**. Write the name of two animals in which the letters ey make the **long** e sound?

The **vowel pair** ie has the **long** i sound, as in p**ie**.

The **vowel digraph** ie can stand for the **long** e sound, as in p**ie**ce.

⭐ **Add** ie **to the letters in the boxes to form words. Then write the words to complete the sentences.**

cr___d
tr___d
sp___d
fr___d

___ie ___

1. This means "attempted." _____

2. This means "cooked in oil."_____

3. This means "wept." _____

4. This means "watched secretly."_____

ch___f
th___f
br___f
gr___f

___ie ___

5. This means "sadness." _____

6. This is a robber. _____

7. This is a leader. _____

8. This means "short." _____

⭐ **Use a word from the box below to complete each sentence.**

pie   believe   shriek   untied   piece   die   dried   achieve

9. To accept as true is to _____.

10. Riding a roller coaster causes most people to _____.

11. Can I have a large _____ of that chocolate cake?

12. To accomplish is to _____.

13. As soon as Dad got home, he _____ his necktie.

14. I placed _____ flowers in a vase.

15. I think apple _____ is my favorite dessert.

16. The plants will _____ if we do not water them.

🏠 **Home Involvement Activity** Recite the old rhyme that helps us remember how to spell some tricky words. *Use i before e, except after c, or when sounded like a, as in n**ei**ghbor and w**ei**gh.*

Name _____

Every **syllable** has a vowel sound. Follow these rules for dividing words into syllables.

- Never divide a one-syllable word.

    thief   sail   cheek   sway   lie   head   Maine

- Never divide long **vowel pairs** or **vowel digraphs.**

    sweat-er   neigh-bor   re-ceive   crea-ture   be-lieve

- Do not split r-controlled vowels.

    arch-er-y   por-tion   ver-dict   cir-cle   bur-den

- If two vowels together make *two* separate sounds, divide them.

    cre-ate   qui-et   re-act   O-hi-o

- Treat y in the middle or at the end of a word as a vowel.

    ver-y   bi-cy-cle   pyr-a-mid   Wy-o-ming

⭐ **Write each word. Use a hyphen (-) to divide the word into syllables. Check the box above to see which rule to use.**

1. fortune _____

2. season _____

3. feature _____

4. people _____

5. bury _____

6. tricycle _____

7. diet _____

8. pioneer _____

Early photograph of a pioneer family

WORD STRATEGY

Divide compound words into syllables by separating the one-syllable words that form them:

    fruit-cake
    broad-cast

List five other compound words. Divide them into syllables.

Here are more rules to help you divide words into syllables.

• If a word has two consonants between two vowels **(VCCV)**, divide between consonants. BUT—do *not* split **consonant blends** or **consonant digraphs**.

sun-ny   fel-low   can-vas   fif-ty   mon-key   ush-er   lath-er

• If a word has one consonant between two vowels **(VCV)**, divide *after* the consonant if the first vowel is short.

shad-ow   nev-er   hab-it   trav-el   riv-er

• If a word has one consonant between two vowels **(VCV)**, divide *before* the consonant if the first vowel is long.

pi-lot   re-gal   ba-sic   o-ver   cra-zy

Write each word. Use a hyphen (-) to divide the word into syllables. Check the box above to see which rule to use.

1. terror _____

2. washer _____

3. pillow _____

4. gravel _____

5. robot _____

6. donkey _____

7. basis _____

8. rabbit _____

9. under _____

10. sixty _____

11. closet _____

12. ever _____

13. wagon _____

14. favor _____

15. rather _____

16. lazy _____

Statue of
Admiral Lord Nelson,
1843

LESSON 21: Syllables with Short and Long Vowels, **r**-controlled Vowels, Vowel Pairs, and Vowel Digraphs

Home Involvement Activity These are the names of three famous ships: the *Pinta*, the *Ranger*, and the *Victoria*. Divide the names into syllables. Then find out about the great captain of each ship.

Name _____

⭐ **Read each group of words. Say and spell each word in bold print. Repeat the word. Then sort the words. Write each word in the correct column below.**

- **explore** the unknown

- **heed** the warning

- a group of **rare** birds

- how **reindeer** survive

- the earth's water **cycle**

- on a **daring** voyage

- **seize** the moment

- in the **chilly** breeze

- **endure** harsh conditions

- a **typical** day

- shaped like a **pyramid**

- a **nature** walk

- might **freeze** solid

- just like **poetry**

- will **remain** for a year

- **disagree** with the leader

Words with r-controlled Vowels	Words with Vowel Pairs or Vowel Digraphs	Words with y as a Vowel

Antarctica is the coldest spot on Earth. Almost all of this continent is covered with ice all year long. No animals or plants can survive there year-round. Yet explorers have risked their lives to learn about this cold and lonely place. Today, people use Antarctica only for scientific research.

Think about why explorers may have risked their lives to go to Antarctica. Write your ideas in a brief essay. End your essay by telling whether you would ever visit this cold, lonely place. Use two or more of these spelling words.

explore   heed   rare   reindeer   cycle   daring

seize   chilly   endure   typical

pyramid   nature   freeze   poetry   remain   disagree

_____

_____

_____

_____

_____

_____

_____

_____

_____

_____

Writer's Tip

Before you begin to write, find out facts about Antarctica in a reference book, such as an atlas. Choose the best information. You can also research Antarctica on the Internet.

Writer's Challenge

Write an eyewitness account to describe what you saw when a group of explorers came to Antarctica. Take the point of view of a penguin who saw the explorers arrive and who watched them struggle. Keep the same point of view throughout.

Name _____

Say the word next to the number. Underline the words in the row that have the same vowel sound as the numbered word.

1	art	heart	dark	chair	steep	worm
2	flat	great	grab	brag	jar	wrap
3	try	my	play	sky	rye	knife
4	whirl	which	squirrel	worried	girl	turn
5	stair	chair	stain	steer	mare	dryer
6	head	greed	leaf	led	health	bread
7	rein	stain	being	plane	veil	height
8	peach	stream	crease	pause	swear	Greek
9	word	born	work	fork	birch	churn
10	sleigh	sway	bright	prey	sweat	clay
11	prune	rule	grape	truce	drum	church
12	form	color	stork	worm	home	porch

Underline the word in each pair that has the same vowel sound as the sound at the beginning of the row.

13. **Long i** thief or pie? rhyme or sixty? speed or spied?

14. **Long e** meat or pearl? early or green? meant or cheat?

15. **Long a** weigh or grieve? peach or paint? sweat or stray?

16. **Short e** break or thread? clear or wealth? bread or braid?

17. **Short i** sprint or sprite? trail or gym? fright or wrist?

18. **Short o** flop or chore? nose or nozzle? low or log?

Fill in the circle of the word that completes each sentence. Then write the word on the line.

1. Christopher Columbus lived for a time in _____.
   ○ Maine   ○ Spain   ○ Baytown

2. He wished to explore unknown parts of the _____.
   ○ weird   ○ whirl   ○ world

3. He hoped to get money to _____ new lands.
   ○ seek   ○ eke   ○ sheik

4. It took more than a _____ to get ready for the voyage.
   ○ week   ○ weak   ○ wreck

5. The journey in 1492 was long and _____.
   ○ heard   ○ herd   ○ hard

6. The crew was thrilled to spot _____ land.
   ○ dray   ○ dried   ○ dry

A *hink-pink* is a pair of one-syllable words that rhyme. Complete each hink-pink with a word that rhymes with the word in bold print. Watch out! Just because the words rhyme doesn't mean that they are spelled alike!

7. If you think too hard, you might get _____ **strain**.

8. I raised a robin. Then I raised a wren. Now I'm raising my

   third _____.

9. The king's wicked wife is called the _____ **queen**.

10. If you fear that your wig will fall off, you'll have a

    _____ **scare**!

Extend & Apply

Make up your own hink-pinks. To help, write at least one rhyming word on each blank line.

11. clay _____   12. head _____

13. dare _____   14. splash _____

Name _____

Helpful Hint

The **vowel digraphs** au and aw stand for the aw sound.
The sound of a in al also makes this sound. Listen:

The artist will draw all through the autumn.

⭐ **Write the letters au, aw, or al to complete each word.**

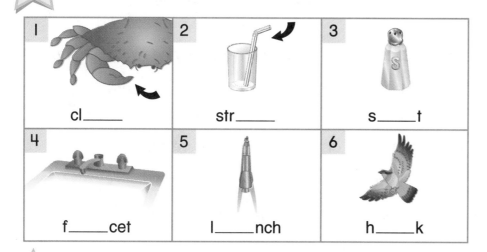

1 cl_____	2 str_____	3 s_____t
4 f_____cet	5 l_____nch	6 h_____k

⭐ **Underline the word that names each picture. Then write the word on the line.**

7 bale bawl ball _____	8 claw crawl paw _____	9 saw straw shawl _____
10 dawn caution yawn _____	11 sauce laundry always _____	12 saucer faucet stall _____

⭐ **Choose two words from the boxes above. Write a sentence using both words.**

13. _____

⭐ **Choose a word from the box to complete each sentence. Write the word on the line. Use the hints in parentheses ( ).**

walking	shawl	sprawled	yawning	caught
launch	dawn	lawn	small	tall	talk

⭐ **Complete each sentence with a word from the box.**

1. The _____ was planned for that Tuesday morning. (rhymes with *staunch*)

2. Everyone was _____ up in the excitement. (rhymes with *taught*)

3. Whenever people got together they would _____ about the mission. (rhymes with *walk*)

4. We left our home early in order to arrive at the launch before _____. (rhymes with *lawn*)

5. Many people were already there, and some were sleepy and _____. (rhymes with *awning*)

6. Others were _____ toward the rocket to get a closer look. (rhymes with *squawking*)

7. Some people were standing, but others were _____ on the grass. (rhymes with *hauled*)

8. A few families spread blankets on the _____ and had breakfast. (rhymes with *fawn*)

9. My mother was cold, so she put on her _____. (rhymes with *ball*)

10. I looked up when the _____ rocket began to lift off. (rhymes with *crawl*)

11. Even _____ children began to cheer. (rhymes with *stall*)

LESSON 24: Vowel Digraphs **au** and **aw; al**

Home Involvement Activity Au**stin, Texas,** is a city that has the vowel digraph **au** in its name. Brainstorm to create a list of other place names that have the vowel digraph **au** or **aw**.

Name _____

Helpful Hint

The **vowel digraph** oo can have two different sounds.
It can stand for the vowel sound you hear in **moon**
or the vowel sound you hear in **book**. Listen:

Read this **book** about exploring the **moon**.

Complete each sentence with a word from the box.
Then *circle* the *moon* (🌙) or the *book* (📖)
to show the oo sound in the word you wrote.

lagoon	looked	cook	food	stood
smooth	swooped	took	shook	drooped

🌙 **1.** We sailed the ship into the _____.

🌙 **2.** A pelican _____ down and landed on the deck.

🌙 **3.** The flag _____ in the hot and still evening.

🌙 **4.** I _____ on deck to watch the sunset.

🌙 **5.** I _____ at the amazing colors in the sky.

🌙 **6.** While there was still light, I _____ a picture.

🌙 **7.** I ate some _____ while on deck.

🌙 **8.** The calm but steady winds made for

_____ sailing.

🌙 **9.** Yet the ship _____ when the
winds picked up.

🌙 **10.** The ship's _____ served dinner
when the sea became calm.

CHALLENGE

Write a long
sentence that
includes words
with the oo vowel
digraph. Here's
an example:
Look in **school**
for **cool boots,**
wooden stools,
or **good books.**

The **vowel pairs** oa and oe have the **long o** sound. Listen:

The **d**oe was startled and darted across the r**oa**d.

⭐ **Use a word from the box to complete each sentence. Write the word on the line.**

tiptoe   croaked   toast   oath   groaned   Monroe   approached   foes

1. The ship slowly _____ the harbor.

2. The large bullfrogs _____ loudly.

3. I had to _____ past the bedroom where the baby slept.

4. I like butter and jam on my _____.

5. Carlos and Paul took the Boy Scout _____.

6. The class _____ when the teacher gave us more homework.

7. We learned that James _____ was the fifth President.

8. Unfortunately, he had many _____ in the government.

⭐ **Combine the letters in the box with the phonogram oat to form words. Use the words to complete the sentences.**

m
fl
thr
g

_____ oat

9. A cow and a _____ give milk.

10. To rest on top of water is to _____.

11. Inside your neck is your _____.

12. Around a castle you'll find a _____.

Home Involvement Activity Underline the vowel pairs in these words: b**oa**t and t**oe**. Then circle the same vowel pairs in an article from your local newspaper.

Name _____

Helpful Hint

A **diphthong** is two vowels blended together as one sound.

The diphthongs oi in f**oi**l and oy in b**oy** have the same vowel sound.

The diphthong ew has the vowel sound in **n**ew.

⭐ **Say** the name of the picture in each box. Then sort the words below. Write each of the words in the correct column.

| dew   annoy   coil   jewel   boy   avoid   oyster   threw   poison |

1 **ew as in**	2 **oi as in**	3 **oy as in**
st**ew**	b**oil**	t**oy**
_____	_____	_____
_____	_____	_____
_____	_____	_____

⭐ **Write a word from the box below to complete each sentence.**

| enjoy   destroy   new |

4. Some explorers see the ocean bottom as a

_____ frontier.

5. Scientists try not to _____ the ocean.

6. Do you _____ learning about underwater explorers?

WORK TOGETHER

Draw a big pot for boiling a silly **st**ew. Work with a group. On the pot, list silly "ingredients." Use words with the oi, oy, and ew diphthongs.

LESSON 26: Diphthongs **oi**, **oy**, **ew**   **55**

Remember: A **diphthong** is two vowels blended together as one sound, as in **d**ew.

⭐ Combine the letters in the boxes with the diphthongs oi, oy, **and** ew **to form words. Use the words to complete the sentences.**

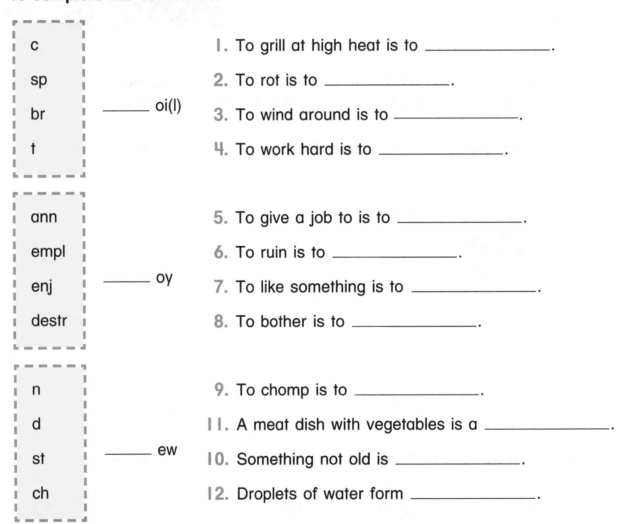

c

sp

br

t

—— oi(l)

1. To grill at high heat is to _____.

2. To rot is to _____.

3. To wind around is to _____.

4. To work hard is to _____.

ann

empl

enj

destr

—— oy

5. To give a job to is to _____.

6. To ruin is to _____.

7. To like something is to _____.

8. To bother is to _____.

n

d

st

ch

—— ew

9. To chomp is to _____.

11. A meat dish with vegetables is a _____.

10. Something not old is _____.

12. Droplets of water form _____.

⭐ **Choose one word from each of the three groups above. Write a sentence for each word.**

13. _____

14. _____

15. _____

Home Involvement Activity Try this tongue twister: "A n**oi**sy n**oi**se ann**oy**s an **oy**ster." Then make up tongue twisters of your own. Use diphthongs.

Name _____

Helpful Hints

The **vowel pair** ow can make the **long o** sound. Listen:

cr**ow**   b**ow**l   sn**ow**

The **diphthong** ow stands for the sound you hear in t**ow**n.

⭐ **Say each word in the box. Then sort the words by the ow sound. Write each word in the correct column.**

1 **pillow**

2 **owl**

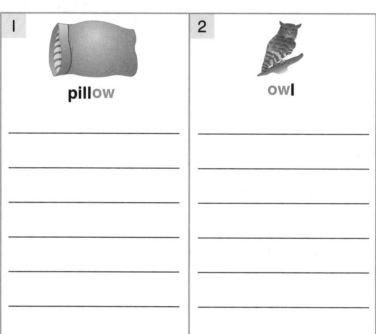

flow	grown
rowdy	sorrow
shower	bowling
allowed	now
plow	yellow
tomorrow	cowboy
browse	borrow
throw	chow

⭐ **Combine the letters in the box with the diphthong ow to form words. Use the words to complete the sentences.**

h
f
gr
pr

___ow(l)

3. A rooster is not fish but _____.

4. To _____ is to make a low sound.

5. To move about secretly is to _____.

6. Wolves _____ at the moon.

WORD STRATEGY

When you read the word **b**ow, how do you know if it's pronounced **b**ow as in **c**ow or **b**ow as in **kn**ow? What about **r**ow and **s**ow? Use context clues when you read to figure out how to say a word.

The **diphthong** ou can have the vowel sound you hear in
pr**ou**d. **Ou** can also have these three other sounds. Listen:
A c**ou**ple of doves th**ou**ght it saw a c**ou**gar on the gr**ou**nd.

⭐ **Read each group of words. Underline the word with ou. Then write the word in the correct column.**

1. had some yummy soup
2. scored a touchdown
3. visit with some cousins
4. had enough to eat
5. joined a rock group
6. flew in rough weather
7. looked for coupons
8. drove through Utah

ou **as in** co**u**gar	ou **as in** co**u**ple
_____	_____
_____	_____
_____	_____
_____	_____

⭐ **Now do the same for these phrases. Read each group of words. Underline the word with ou. Then write the word in the correct column.**

9. lives in a large house
10. fought for freedom
11. ought to win
12. kept in a pouch
13. climbed the mountain
14. bought some clothes
15. sought a new job
16. had many doubts

ou **as in** tr**ou**t	ou **as in** c**ou**gh
_____	_____
_____	_____
_____	_____
_____	_____

Home Involvement Activity Take turns reading this
sentence: "Take y**ou**r stars on t**ou**r." When r follows ou,
it can make another sound. Write three sentences that
use words with this sound.

Name _____

Here are more rules to help you divide words into syllables.
Notice that these words have **vowel pairs, vowel digraphs,**
or **diphthongs.**

• Never divide long vowels or the broad o digraphs au or aw.

fea-ture   stee-ple   dai-sy   goat-ee   au-di-ence   draw-ing

• Never divide diphthongs or the vowel digraph oo.

thou-sand   poi-son   tow-er   roy-al

floun-der   jew-el   school-book   coop-er

Write each word. Divide it into syllables by using a hyphen (-).
Check the box above to see which rule to use.

1. creature _____

2. faucet _____

3. raccoon _____

4. bookworm _____

5. container _____

6. awful _____

7. seizure _____

8. auditions _____

9. groaning _____

10. sleepwalk _____

11. ointment _____

12. cheapen _____

13. brawny _____

14. viewpoint _____

15. flower _____

16. doubtful _____

17. sawdust _____

18. teaspoon _____

19. voyage _____

20. naughty _____

21. rowdy _____

22. pouncing _____

CHALLENGE

Try to divide these
long words. Use
a dictionary, if
needed.

cautiousness

whereabouts

entertainment

Don't let your eyes fool you about syllables. You need to look *and* listen. Complete the chart. The first one has been done for you.

Word	Vowels I See	Vowel Sounds I Hear	Number of Syllables
1 headache	4	2	2
2 seizure			
3 willow			
4 moonbeam			
5 newspaper			
6 toenail			
7 treatment			
8 houseplant			
9 applesauce			
10 mountain			
11 nosebleed			
12 embroider			

Here are the names of some famous explorers. Divide their last names into syllables.

13. Matthew **Henson** _____

14. John **Cabot** _____

15. Ferdinand **Magellan** _____

16. Mary **Kingsley** _____

17. Marco **Polo** _____

18. Leif **Ericson** _____

Matthew Henson (1866–1955) reached the North Pole with Robert Peary in 1909.

LESSON 28: Syllables with Vowel Pairs, Vowel Digraphs, and Diphthongs

Home Involvement Activity Find out about one or more of the explorers above. Use the Internet, an encyclopedia, or a social studies book. Share what you learn.

Name _____

★ **Read about Sylvia Earle, an underwater explorer. Then answer the questions that follow.**

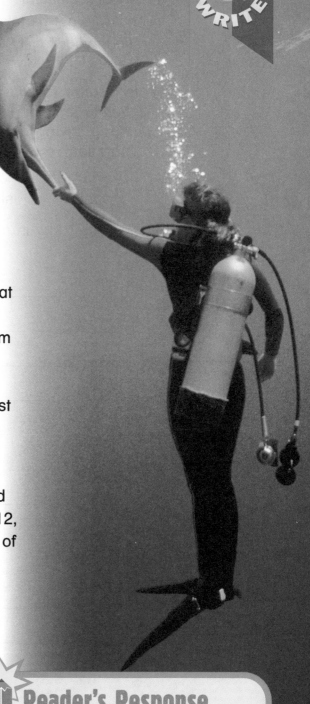

Meet an Underwater Explorer

by Luise Woelflein

Sylvia Earle has spent more than 6,000 hours under water. She has played around with friendly dolphins. She has gotten "personal" with animals that can be dangerous, such as sharks and moray eels. She has studied humpback whales by following them under water.

Sylvia is a *marine biologist*—a scientist who studies ocean life. She's also one of the world's best underwater divers. Being an ocean scientist and an underwater diver fit right together. Sylvia can study life in the ocean—as it's happening.

Ever since she was a little girl, Sylvia has looked for ways to get under water. Then, when she was 12, her family moved to Florida. Sylvia spent hundreds of hours playing there in the warm, clear water of the Gulf of Mexico.

When Sylvia got to college, she tried out scuba gear for the first time. (Scuba gear is equipment for breathing under water.) "It was glorious!" she says. "It was like being a fish. My professor almost had to haul me out of the water by force, I liked it so much."

It's still hard to get Sylvia out of the water. In fact, she wants lots of people to learn how to explore the ocean. Why? Because so little is known about what's there.

🔖 Reader's Response

1. **What do underwater explorers like Sylvia do?**

2. **Do you think their work is important? Why?**

3. **Would you like to be an underwater explorer someday? Give reasons for your decision.**

Imagine that you have been invited to explore the ocean with an underwater explorer. You have decided that you want to go, but you will have to get permission from your family. What will you say to persuade your family to let you go?

Write a letter to your parent or guardian. Try to persuade him or her to let you explore the ocean with a real scientist. Give three strong reasons for letting you go. Use some of these persuasive words to make your reasons more convincing.

ought	should	must	believe	think
feel	in my opinion		important	opportunity

_____

_____

_____

_____

Writer's Tip

Words such as *ought* and *should* will help to persuade your audience.

_____

_____

_____

_____

_____

_____

_____

Speaker's Challenge

Give your letter as a speech to your class. Try to persuade your listeners to agree with your point of view.

LESSON 29: Connecting Reading and Writing Comprehension—Make Decisions; Synthesize

Say the word next to the number. Then circle the letter before the word in each row that has the same vowel sound as the letters in red.

1. feather   a. peaceful   b. measure   c. seasons

2. saucer   a. yawn   b. mouse   c. thousand

3. smooth   a. bookmark   b. crooked   c. raccoon

4. whirl   a. awhile   b. pear   c. word

5. tiptoe   a. approach   b. baboon   c. haunted

6. cloudy   a. shawl   b. showed   c. rowdy

7. stall   a. gallon   b. faucet   c. talent

8. avoid   a. await   b. annoyed   c. violin

9. book   a. took   b. lucky   c. harpoon

10. reins   a. sleigh   b. ceiling   c. diet

Read each sentence. Choose the letter pair from the three in each row that completes both unfinished words. Write the same letters from the chart in both spaces.

au	aw	al
ea	ee	ei
ea	ee	ie
ie	ee	ea
au	oa	oe
au	oa	ea
ew	ow	oo
oy	oa	oi
ea	ou	au

11. We _____ways add s_____t to our mashed potatoes.

12. Do you agr_____ that this color s_____ms too pale?

13. Matt left his j_____ns in a h_____p on the floor.

14. When we saw the th_____f, we shr_____ked in fear.

15. It hurts to eat t_____st when you have a sore thr_____t.

16. Dad's old sw_____ter has l_____ther buttons.

17. Karla thr_____ some peanuts into the st_____.

18. She likes to embr_____der with turqu_____se thread.

19. The t_____r of West Africa included y_____r village.

Read about a courageous woman explorer. For each numbered blank, there is a choice of words below. Circle the letter before the word that best completes the sentence.

Do you think that all explorers are men? Well, think again. Some women took scary **1**, too. They had **2** adventures that still thrill us. One of these women was Mary Kingsley. Mary explored Africa in the 1890s. And she did it in a dress!

As a child, Mary read her father's travel books. She **3** said that his books opened up new worlds to her. Mary's father loved the bright eyes of danger. Maybe she had **4** because of the words he wrote about all his adventures.

Some explorers try to conquer the people they meet—but not Mary Kingsley. She went to parts of western and central Africa where Europeans had never been before. She lived with the local people. She **5** respect for their ways. Today, people still read about Mary Kingsley's **6** to adventure.

1. **a.** views **b.** voyages **c.** voices
2. **a.** awesome **b.** dawn **c.** crooked
3. **a.** never **b.** rarely **c.** always
4. **a.** bounce **b.** courage **c.** cougar
5. **a.** showed **b.** groaned **c.** shouted
6. **a.** flow **b.** boast **c.** road

Read the passage again to answer these questions. Circle the letter of the correct answer.

7. As an explorer, Mary Kinglsey
   a. was cautious
   b. visited schools
   c. lived with the local people
   d. fought dangerous animals

8. In the third paragraph, the word **conquer** means—
   a. imitate
   b. defeat
   c. yield to
   d. hunt

Extend & Apply

What could it mean to love "the bright eyes of danger"? Explain how it may have led Mary Kingsley to become an explorer.

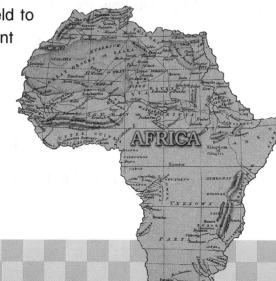
AFRICA

An American Artist

The United States has produced many great artists and composers. Read about one American artist who became famous at the age of 100!

Do you know the saying "better late than never"? These words fit the life of Grandma Moses. Like some well-known artists and composers, Grandma Moses did not become famous until late in her life. However, she did not begin painting until she was in her seventies. Imagine that!

Grandma Moses's real name was Anna Mary Robertson Moses. She was born in upstate New York in 1860. Grandma Moses had no real art training. Yet once she began painting, nothing could stop her. Her subject was the small-town life she knew and loved. She was still painting at the age of 100! By then, Grandma Moses was a household name.

Grandma Moses's fame began to grow in 1940. That's when she had her first art show in New York City. She was 80 years old! Her paintings delighted art lovers. They were amazed by the many details. People liked her happy, colorful scenes.

Grandma Moses's fame made people notice the joy of American art. Today, Americans can thank her for being a true American artist.

Critical Thinking

1. Why are the paintings of Grandma Moses so popular?

2. What do you like about Grandma Moses's painting at the top of the page?

3. If you were to give this painting a caption, what would you write?

**Visit us at
www.sadlier-oxford.com**

UNIT 3
Artists and Composers

An American Artist

The United States has produced many great artists and composers. Read about one American artist who became famous at the age of 100!

Do you know the saying "better late than never"? These words fit the life of Grandma Moses. Like some well-known artists and composers, Grandma Moses did not become famous until late in her life. However, she did not begin painting until she was in her seventies. Imagine that!

Grandma Moses's real name was Anna Mary Robertson Moses. She was born in upstate New York in 1860. Grandma Moses had no real art training. Yet once she began painting, nothing could stop her. Her subject was the small-town life she knew and loved. She was still painting at the age of 100! By then, Grandma Moses was a household name.

Grandma Moses's fame began to grow in 1940. That's when she had her first art show in New York City. She was 80 years old! Her paintings delighted art lovers. They were amazed by the many details. People liked her happy, colorful scenes.

Grandma Moses's fame made people notice the joy of American art. Today, Americans can thank her for being a true American artist.

Critical Thinking

1. Why are the paintings of Grandma Moses so popular?
2. What do you like about Grandma Moses's painting at the top of the page?
3. If you were to give this painting a caption, what would you write?

LESSON 31: Introduction to Word Endings, Contractions, Plurals, Possessives, and Compound Words 65

Dear Family,

In Unit 3, your child will explore and use word endings, contractions, plurals, possessives, and compound words. The theme of this unit is *artists and composers*.

A **contraction** is a word that usually combines two words by leaving out one or more letters. An **apostrophe** (') shows where a letter or letters have been left out. Some examples of contractions are **I'm** (*I am*), **don't** (*do not*), and **aren't** (*are not*).

A **possessive noun** shows who or what has or owns something. An **apostrophe** and an **s** ('s) are used to form a singular possessive noun (the **artist's** painting).

A **compound word** is made up of two or more smaller words. Your child often uses compound words, such as **classroom** and **homework**.

Family Focus

- Work together to create a "family" work of art. You might make a family tree or a family crest. You might create a mural, a collage, a photograph album, or a scrapbook to celebrate your family.

- Visit a local art museum. Look for paintings by Grandma Moses and by other American artists. Discuss what these artists have in common. Then talk about their differences.

- Attend a concert with your family or listen to CDs or tapes. Talk about what you liked most about the music.

LINKS TO LEARNING

To extend learning together, you might explore:

Web Sites
www.benningtonmuseum.com
www.metmuseum.org

CDs
An American Celebration, New York Philharmonic, 10-CD set.

Videos
The Famous Composers Series, PBS Home Video, 10 videos.

Sister Wendy's Story of Painting, PBS Home Video, 5 videos.

Literature
Grandma Moses by Tom Biracree, ©1989.

Name _____

Helpful Hint

Add **s**, **ed**, or **ing** to most **base words** to make a new word.

ask + s = asks   ask + ed = asked

ask + ing = asking

⭐ **Add s, ed, and ing to each base word. Write the new words on the lines.**

		Add s	Add ed	Add ing
1	paint			
2	look			
3	turn			
4	perform			

Ballerina and Lady with Fan by Edgar Degas

Helpful Hint

Add **es** to words that end in **s**, **ss**, **ch**, **sh**, **x**, **z**, or **zz**.

guess + **es** = guesses   beach + **es** = beaches

⭐ **Add es to the words in the box below to complete each sentence. Write the new words on the lines.**

> fix   splash   sketch   waltz

5. The artist either _____ or paints the ballet dancers.

6. He _____ paint on the canvas.

7. The piano tuner also _____ harps.

8. The dancer _____ to the tunes on the radio.

CHALLENGE

Use the spelling strategies you have just learned to add **s** or **es**, **ed**, and **ing** to the base words below. Then write a sentence for each new word you write.

box
boss
buzz

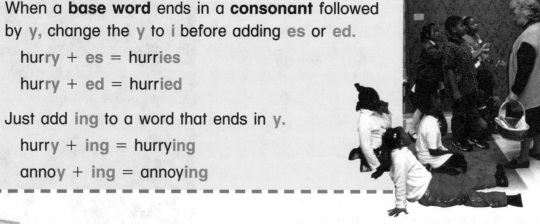

When a **base word** ends in a **consonant** followed by **y**, change the **y** to **i** before adding **es** or **ed**.

hur**ry** + **es** = hurr**ies**

hur**ry** + **ed** = hurr**ied**

Just add **ing** to a word that ends in **y**.

hurr**y** + **ing** = hurry**ing**

anno**y** + **ing** = annoy**ing**

⭐ **Add** s or es, ed, **and** ing **to each base word. Change** y **to** i **as needed. Write the new words on the lines.**

		Add s or es	Add ed	Add ing
1	dry			
2	carry			
3	deny			
4	study			
5	play			

⭐ **Add** s or es, ed, **or** ing **to each word in bold print so that the sentence makes sense. Write the new words on the lines.**

6. Danny **visit** the art museum earlier today. _____

7. Right now, a guide is **try** to explain oil painting. _____

8. The class was **listen** closely to her. _____

9. At this moment, Danny **want** to be an artist. _____

10. After he **finish** his homework, he will create his first painting. _____

11. He is **think** of a circus scene. _____

12. Danny **study** some drawings about an hour ago. _____

Home Involvement Activity Cut and **put** are words that are the same in the present and the past tense. Work together to write a brief list of words that do not change from the present to the past.

Name _____

Helpful Hints

When a **base word** ends in **silent** e, drop the **final** e before adding ed or ing.

    dance + ed = danced   dance + ing = dancing

For most words ending in silent e, keep the e when adding s.

    dance + s = dances

Add s, ed, **and** ing **to each base word below.**
Write the new words in the chart.

		Add s	Add ed	Add ing
1	wave			
2	skate			
3	trace			
4	erase			
5	practice			
6	glide			
7	exercise			
8	describe			
9	bake			
10	divide			

Write the base word for each word below.

11. moves _____

12. tuned _____

13. writing _____

14. pronounced _____

15. traded _____

16. losing _____

CHALLENGE

Change the headlines in a newspaper so that the verbs end in s or es, ed, or ing. Make needed spelling changes.

When a **base word** with one syllable ends in one **vowel** followed by a **consonant,** usually double the final consonant before adding ed or ing.

clap + ed = clapped   clap + ing = clapping

For most two-syllable words ending in one vowel and one consonant, double the consonant only if the accent is on the second syllable.

admit + ed = admitted   admit + ing = admitting

Add ed or ing to each base word. Double the final consonant as needed. Write the new words in the chart.

	Add ed	Add ing
1 shop		
2 rob		
3 permit		
4 plan		

Complete the passage by adding ed or ing to the base words in the box. Write the new words on the lines.

| spot | study | use | lead | focus | show |

Jacob Lawrence was born in 1917. He grew up in New York City.

There he **(5)** _____ art. His teachers **(6)** _____ his talent right

away. In his paintings, Lawrence **(7)** _____

bright colors and flat shapes. He also **(8)** _____

on painting African American heroes. For example,

he did a series of paintings of Harriet Tubman.

He **(9)** _____ her **(10)** _____ enslaved

people to freedom on the Underground Railroad.

Forward by Jacob Lawrence, 1967

Home Involvement Activity The words **flow** and **show** do not fit the double-the-final-consonant rule. For these words, you just add ed or ing. What other one-syllable words are like these? Make a list.

Name _____

Helpful Hint

A **contraction** usually combines two words into one. In a contraction, one or more letters have been left out. An **apostrophe** (') shows where the missing letter or letters were.

does + not = **doesn't**   it + is = **it's**   would + not = **wouldn't**

I + have = **I've**   she + would = **she'd**   he + will = **he'll**

Write the contraction for each pair of words. Use the contractions from the box. Then write the letter or letters that have been left out of each contraction.

can't	we'll	let's	aren't	you've

		Contraction	Letter(s) Left Out
1	we will		
2	are not		
3	let us		
4	you have		
5	cannot		

WORK TOGETHER

Work with a group to write a different contraction on each of ten index cards. Take turns picking cards. Tell your group the two words that make up the contraction on each card you pick.

Underline the contraction in each sentence. Then write the two words it stands for.

6. Georgia O'Keeffe always knew she'd be

   a painter. _____ _____

7. She wouldn't let anything stop her.

   _____ _____

8. You'll love her colorful paintings

   of flowers. _____ _____

Red Canna
by Georgia O'Keeffe,
1924

⭐ **Read the words. Write their contractions on the lines.**

1. we have _____

2. they are _____

3. he is _____

4. does not _____

5. she will _____

6. do not _____

7. that is _____

8. cannot _____

9. they have _____

10. they will _____

11. I have _____

12. we will _____

13. is not _____

14. would not _____

15. I would _____

16. could not _____

17. was not _____

18. should not _____

19. you are _____

20. he would _____

⭐ **These song titles should have contractions. Rewrite each title by using a contraction.**

21. "I Have Been a Fool"

_____

22. "Let Us Dance"

_____

23. "We Are in the Money"

_____

24. "Would Not It Be Nice?"

_____

25. "Why Cannot You Behave?"

_____

26. "You Are Still the One"

_____

 Home Involvement Activity Create a list of songs that have contractions in the title. Work together to replace each contraction with the words for which it stands.

Name _____

⭐ **Read each group of words. Say and spell each word in bold print. Repeat the word. Then sort the words. Write the words correctly in the boxes below.**

- **doesn't** have a partner
- **practicing** the piano
- heard the **buzzing**
- **chatting** all day
- never **tried** tap dancing
- began **showing** the pictures
- on the **planning** committee
- **listens** to the orchestra

- **reaches** for the brush
- **isn't** in the band
- **carries** a violin case
- **played** the harp
- **scrubbed** the chalkboard
- **describing** the photograph
- **shouldn't** talk during the concert
- **danced** to the music

Drop Final e

| |
| |
| |

Change y to i

| |
| |

No Base Changes

| |
| |
| |
| |
| |

Double Final Consonant

| |
| |
| |

Has a Contraction

| |
| |
| |

Choose a song that you know and like. Imagine that you are going to teach it to a friend. Think about the best way to teach your friend the song.

Write a list of the steps you would follow to teach a song to your friend. Put the steps in the order that makes the most sense. Use at least three of these spelling words.

doesn't	practicing	buzzing	chatting	tried	showing
planning	listens	reaches	isn't	carries	
played	scrubbed	describing	shouldn't	danced	

_____

_____

_____

_____

_____

_____

_____

_____

_____

_____

_____

_____

Writer's Tips

First, list all the steps on a separate sheet of paper. Next, arrange the steps in order by numbering them. If you've left anything out, now is the time to add it. Finally, write your steps on this page.

Writer's Challenge

Think about a game or a sport that you know how to play. How would you teach this game to someone who had never played it? First, list the steps of the game in order. Then write a paragraph explaining how to play the game.

Name _____

Helpful Hint

Plural means "more than one." To make most **base words** plural, add **s**.

    band + **s** = band**s**   stage + **s** = stage**s**

Add **es** to words that end in **s, ss, ch, sh, x, z,** or **zz**.

    dress + **es** = dress**es**   inch + **es** = inch**es**
    bru**sh** + **es** = brush**es**   bo**x** + **es** = box**es**

CHALLENGE

Make a list of ten songs, stories, books, or movies that have plural words in their titles. Here are some ideas:

101 Dalmations
The Three Wishes

Circle each plural word on your list.

⭐ **Add s or es to form the plural of each word. Write the plural word on the line.**

1. song _____

2. concert _____

3. tax _____

4. violin _____

5. flute _____

6. porch _____

7. waltz _____

8. fizz _____

9. genius _____

10. mix _____

11. princess _____

12. bush _____

⭐ **Add s or es to each word in bold print so that the sentence makes sense. Write the new word on the line.**

13. Darla is one of the **sculptor** in my art class.

    _____

14. Most of her sculptures are of **athlete**.

    _____

15. Two of them show **coach** working with

    students. _____

16. Wayne's **sketch** are the best in the class.

    _____

Helpful Hint

When a **base word** ends in a **consonant** followed by **y**, change the **y** to **i** before adding **es**.

city + es = cities   pastry + es = pastries

When a base word ends in a vowel and **y**, keep the **y** and just add **s**.

play + s = plays   toy + s = toys

Write the plural of each of these base words.

1. monkey _____ 2. melody _____

3. county _____ 4. diary _____

5. berry _____ 6. journey _____

Use a word from the box for each clue. Write one letter in each space. Read down the shaded column to answer the question.

| coins | medleys | adventures | buddies |
| bunches | plays | couches | tubas |

7. performances in a theater   _ _ _ _ _

8. large wind instruments   _ _ _ _ _

9. exciting experiences   _ _ _ _ _ _ _ _ _ _

10. pennies, nickels, dimes, quarters   _ _ _ _ _

11. music made from different songs   _ _ _ _ _ _ _

12. groups of similar things   _ _ _ _ _ _ _

13. sofas   _ _ _ _ _ _ _

14. good friends   _ _ _ _ _ _ _

Question: What do you call the people who come to a concert?

Answer: the _____

Home Involvement Activity Play a game. One person says, "One [any **A** word]." The next player says, "Two [plural of that word]." (*One ax, two axes*) Continue with a **B** word, then a **C** word, and so on, through the alphabet.

Name _____

Helpful Hints

For most words ending in **f**, **lf**, or **fe**, form the plural by changing the **f** to **v** and adding **es**.

leaf = lea**ves**   cal**f** = cal**ves**   li**fe** = li**ves**

There are some exceptions to this rule. Form the plural of some words that end in **f** and all words ending in **ff** by adding **s**.

roo**f** = roo**fs**   chie**f** = chie**fs**   cli**ff** = cli**ffs**

★ **Write the plural form of each word. Look in a dictionary if you need help.**

1. chef _____   2. thief _____

3. half _____   4. knife _____

5. elf _____   6. clef _____

7. cuff _____   8. shelf _____

9. wife _____   10. muff _____

CHALLENGE

Work backward. Write the singular form of the plural words below. Then write a sentence for each word in its singular form.

scarves
wharves
hooves

★ **Complete each sentence with a word from the box below. Use the plural form of each word.**

| wolf | belief | life | loaf |

11. There are two _____ of bread in the basket.

12. In "Little Red Riding Hood" _____ are villains.

13. Many children's _____ are formed at a young age.

14. Do you believe that a cat has nine _____?

Helpful Hints

For most words ending in **o** after a vowel, add **s** to form the plural.

vide**o** + **s** = vide**os**   radi**o** + **s** = radi**os**

For most words ending in **o** after a consonant, add **es** to form the plural.

pota**to** + **es** = potat**oes**   her**o** + **es** = her**oes**

For many music words ending in **o** from the Italian language, just add **s**.

pian**o** = pian**os**   cell**o** = cell**os**

Write the plural form of each word. If you aren't sure whether to add s or es, check a dictionary.

1. tomato _____   2. igloo _____

3. stereo _____   4. studio _____

5. oboe _____   6. soprano _____

7. echo _____   8. trio _____

Write the plural form of each of the eight words below. Then find and circle these eight plural words in the puzzle. The words can go across, on a slant, or up and down.

9. wife _____

10. loaf _____

11. shelf _____

12. thief _____

13. knife _____

14. solo _____

15. rodeo _____

16. piano _____

s	o	l	o	s	t	w	s	e
t	a	r	e	w	p	e	a	v
h	i	v	k	n	i	v	e	s
i	l	e	l	o	a	v	e	s
e	a	r	s	a	n	v	e	t
v	r	o	d	e	o	s	p	s
e	a	h	g	o	s	t	u	e
s	o	s	h	e	l	v	e	s

LESSON 37: Plurals with **f, lf, fe, ff,** and **o**

Home Involvement Activity The following plural music words are scrambled. Unscramble the words. Then place them on a word map, with the word *music* in the center.

inaspo   tosal   ospnrsoa   sleocl   sloos

Name _____

Helpful Hints

The **plurals** of some words do not have **s** or **es** at the end.
These words become plural in irregular ways.

mouse → **mice**   child → **children**   tooth → **teeth**   goose → **geese**

Some words stay the same when singular or plural.

sheep   deer   elk   salmon   moose   series   cattle

Look at the plural forms in the box below. Write each plural next to its singular form.

moose	men	oxen	geese	women
oases	feet	mice	bison	children

1. woman _____
2. foot _____
3. child _____
4. man _____
5. oasis _____
6. mouse _____
7. moose _____
8. ox _____
9. bison _____
10. goose _____

Complete each sentence by using the plural form of the word in the box.

trout	tooth	Child	deer	series

11. Dogs have sharp canine _____.

12. _____ can get into the movies for half price.

13. We caught several _____ in Lake Ward.

14. There are twelve new TV comedy _____.

15. The _____ darted across the country road.

WORD STRATEGY

Some words, such as **deer** and **sheep**, have the *same* singular and plural form. Use context clues when reading to figure out whether the word means "one" or "more than one" in a sentence.

Each clue for this crossword puzzle is given in singular form. Write the plural form in the boxes to solve the crossword puzzle.

Across

1. series	15. ox	26. melody
4. crowd	16. spray	27. oasis
5. cattle	17. chance	28. igloo
6. waltz	18. deer	29. inch
9. knife	19. hen	30. solo
12. piano	23. elk	

Down

1. self	8. wish	21. zero
2. donkey	10. video	22. wife
3. bean	11. story	24. key
5. canvas	13. studio	25. dog
6. woman	14. echo	
7. tax	20. bison	

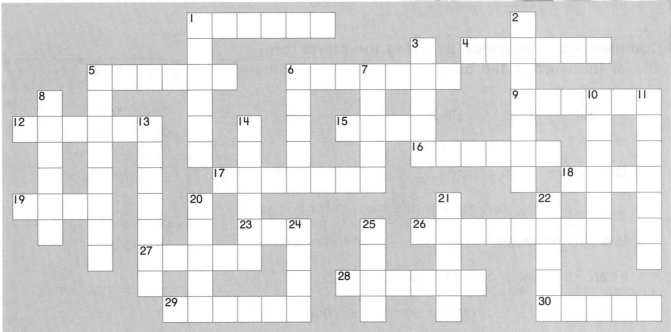

Home Involvement Activity Make up small word-search puzzles that include irregular plurals, such as **teeth** and **feet**. Write your words across, on a slant, or up and down. Then exchange and solve each other's puzzles.

Name _____

★ **Read about a famous American composer. Then answer the questions that follow.**

An American Composer

Aaron Copland was a great American composer. You may not know his name, but you probably have heard his music. Copland was born in 1900 in New York City. Like Grandma Moses, he lived a very long life. Yet unlike her, Copland began studying what he loved at a young age. His music teachers heard his talent right away.

Like many children of immigrants, Copland loved the adventure stories of the American West. In fact, many of his best ideas came from the Wild West or from American folk music. His music for the ballets, *Billy the Kid*, *Rodeo*, and *Appalachian Spring*, are filled with the spirit of the West.

Throughout his career, Copland wrote music for large and small orchestras. He even wrote music for the movies. Copland would find popular tunes that he liked. Then he would use them to build works of great music. For example, he once started with an old Southern lullaby. He then arranged the music for a small orchestra and a solo voice. Today, people still like to pick out popular tunes that they hear in Copland's classical music.

Reader's Response

1. **What makes Aaron Copland a great American composer?**

2. **How are Aaron Copland and Grandma Moses alike? How are they different?**

3. **Would you like to hear some of Aaron Copland's music? Explain your reasons.**

Aaron Copland once used a Southern lullaby to build a piece of great music. You may know the lullaby. It begins:

Hush-a-bye, don't you cry,
Go to sleep, you little baby.

Now it's your turn. Imagine singing a baby to sleep. Write words to your own lullaby. Use at least one pair of the rhymes below to help you write your song.

close	head	sleep	eyes	night	hush	smooth
doze	bed	sheep	rise	light	rush	soothe

Writer's Tips

Use rhyming pairs to write your lullaby.

Also, think about the soothing music that would put a baby to sleep.

_____

_____

_____

_____

_____

_____

_____

_____

_____

_____

Speaker's Challenge

Tell how you wrote your lullaby. Then sing your lullaby to a small group of classmates. Did anybody get sleepy?

Name _____

⭐ **Add s or es, ed, or ing to each base word. Write the new words in the chart. Remember to make spelling changes as needed.**

		Add s or es	Add ed	Add ing
1	dress			
2	attach			
3	mix			
4	buzz			
5	splash			
6	dry			
7	play			
8	dance			
9	clap			
10	admit			

⭐ **Write the base word for each word below.**

11. brushes _____   12. planning _____

13. waved _____   14. sketching _____

15. diaries _____   16. tracing _____

⭐ **Add ed or ing to the base word in the box to complete each sentence.**

```
hope

put

have

practice
```

17. My chorus is _____ on a concert tomorrow.

18. We have been _____ for three months.

19. We are _____ to sing a Russian song.

20. We look forward to _____ you in the audience.

Write the correct plural form of the words below.

1. tax _____   2. salmon _____

3. wife _____   4. stereo _____

5. woman _____   6. shelf _____

7. foot _____   8. tooth _____

Choose the pair of words that make up each contraction in the sentence. Fill in the circle of your answer.

9. I shouldn't be late.   ○ should have   ○ should not   ○ shall not

10. He could've called.   ○ could not   ○ should have   ○ could have

11. You're a great singer.   ○ You will   ○ You were   ○ You are

12. She doesn't dance.   ○ does not   ○ do not   ○ did not

13. It's time to start.   ○ It has   ○ It is   ○ It was

Read the sentences. Fill in the circle of the word that correctly completes each sentence. Then write the word on the line.

14. One of the world's oldest flutes still _____ music.
    ○ play   ○ plays   ○ playing

15. There are similar instruments, but _____ too fragile to use.
    ○ they're   ○ their   ○ there

16. This ancient flute has been around for _____.
    ○ century   ○ centurys   ○ centuries

17. Such flutes were made from the bones of _____.
    ○ animals   ○ animal   ○ animal's

18. The flute is about nine _____ long and has a few small holes.
    ○ inchs   ○ inch   ○ inches

Extend & Apply

How do you think the ancient flute might have been played? Write your answer in a short "how-to" paragraph. Use two plural words.

An ancient flute

Name _____

Helpful Hint

Add an **apostrophe** and an **s** (**'s**) to the end of a singular noun to show who or what has or owns something.

the tool that Scott owns = Scott**'s** tool

the thoughts of one student = one student**'s** thoughts

the guitar that Chris has = Chris**'s** guitar

Rewrite each phrase. Add 's to the word in bold print to show who or what has or owns something.

1. the easel that belongs to **Juan** _____

2. the music book that **Emily** has _____

3. the hands of a **conductor** _____

4. the piano of **Charles** _____

5. the trumpet of the **orchestra** _____

6. the ideas of this **composer** _____

7. the studio that the **artist** owns _____

8. the statue of that **sculptor** _____

Write the possessive form of each word.

9. friend _____ 10. painter _____

11. teacher _____ 12. man _____

13. coach _____ 14. Mr. Lee _____

15. doctor _____ 16. woman _____

17. dancer _____ 18. city _____

19. child _____ 20. mayor _____

21. musician _____ 22. James _____

WORK TOGETHER

Many place names are named for their owners or settlers. Sutter's Mill in California, once owned by Mr. Sutter, is one example. With a partner, list place names that use the possessive form. Use a map to help.

Underline the eight phrases that show who or what has or owns something. Then write a sentence for each phrase.

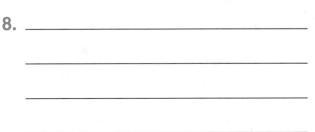

Greg's music book　　　two harps　　　the band's music

the writer's play　　　the girl's crayons　　　pieces of music

the artist's paintings　　　the actors　　　Kevin's paints

the singer's performance　　　sheets of music　　　the city's theaters

1. _____

_____

2. _____

_____

3. _____

_____

4. _____

_____

5. _____

_____

6. _____

_____

7. _____

_____

8. _____

_____

_____

The Migration of the Negro, Panel No. 1, by Jacob Lawrence 1940–1941

Home Involvement Activity Choose one of these creative people. Discuss how the person used art or music to show what was meaningful to him or her.
Grandma Moses　Jacob Lawrence　Aaron Copland

Name _____

Helpful Hints

Add only an **apostrophe** (') to form the **possessive** of a plural noun that ends in **s**.

the cameras that belong to the students = the student**s**' cameras

Add an **apostrophe** and an **s** ('**s**) to form the possessive of a plural noun that does not end in **s**.

the chorus of the women = the women'**s** chorus

the voices of the men = the men'**s** voices

the band of the children = the children'**s** band

Rewrite each phrase. Add an apostrophe (') or an apostrophe and an s ('s) to the word in bold print to show who has or owns something.

1. the pictures that belong to my **friends** _____

2. the books that my **classmates** have _____

3. the games of the **children** _____

4. the classes of the **teachers** _____

5. the room of my **brothers** _____

6. the sketches of the **artists** _____

7. the chorus of the **men** _____

Write the possessive form of these plural words.

8. women _____   9. girls _____

10. doctors _____   11. singers _____

12. cities _____   13. animals _____

14. sisters _____   15. boys _____

16. babies _____   17. tourists _____

CHALLENGE

Change each of these words to its plural form. Then write the possessive form of each plural word.

country

parent

wife

Read each phrase. If the words show that one person has or owns something, write the word *one*. If the words show that more than one person has or owns something, write the words *more than one*.

1. the dancers' performance _____

2. the comic's jokes _____

3. the singer's solo _____

4. the actors' play _____

5. the owners' theater _____

6. the pianist's fingers _____

7. the writer's books _____

8. the painters' mural _____

Read the sentences about the artist Winslow Homer. Fill in the circle of the word that completes each sentence correctly. Then write the word on the line.

9. Winslow Homer was one of the _____ greatest painters.
   ○ country's   ○ countries   ○ countries'

10. His many Civil War _____ made him famous.
    ○ drawings   ○ drawing's   ○ drawings'

11. Homer made sketches of _____ lives.
    ○ soldiers   ○ soldier's   ○ soldiers'

12. These sketches were true _____ of art.
    ○ works   ○ work's   ○ works'

13. The artist was moved by the young

    _____ shyness.
    ○ man   ○ mens   ○ men's

14. His _____ of the sea are also famous.
    ○ picture's   ○ pictures   ○ pictures'

15. Homer made large _____ from some of his sketches.
    ○ paintings   ○ painting's   ○ paintings'

Drum and Bugle Corps, Civil War Encampment by Winslow Homer, 1865

Home Involvement Activity Use each pair of words in the same sentence. Make sure your sentences make sense. Remember not to confuse plurals and possessives.
painters/painters'   friends/friends'

Name _____

Read each group of words. Say and spell each word in bold print. Repeat the word. Then sort the words. Write the words correctly in the boxes below.

- in the **pupils'** interest
- the **children** in my school
- meeting in the **hallways**
- **cities** in our state
- **keys** to success
- one of their **beliefs**
- important to our **lives**
- the **neighborhood's** population

- at work in their **studios**
- the **artist's** drawing
- the **women** of our town
- among our **heroes**
- those **teachers'** classes
- from the highest **branches**
- one of its many **mysteries**
- purchase new **supplies**

Add s or es

Irregular Plurals

Singular Possessives

Plurals for Words That End in f, lf, fe, ff, or o

Drop y, add ies

Plural Possessives

How would you feel if the music and art programs at your school were canceled? What would you do about it? You could write a letter to the editor of your local newspaper. What would you say? How would you persuade people to save these programs at your school?

Write a letter to the editor of your local newspaper. Give three strong reasons for keeping the art and music programs open at your school. Try to convince your audience that these programs are important. Use two or more of these spelling words.

pupils'	children	hallways	cities	keys	beliefs
lives	neighborhood's	studios	artist's	women
heroes	teachers'	branches	mysteries	supplies

Dear Editor: _____

_____

_____

_____

_____

_____

_____

_____

_____

_____

_____

Writer's Tips

State the main idea of your letter right away. Then support it with strong reasons or details. Persuade your readers to agree with you.

Speaker's Challenge

Give your letter as a speech. Use persuasive words, a strong tone of voice, and eye contact to get your audience to agree with your point of view.

Name _____

> **Helpful Hint**

A **compound word** is made up of two or more smaller words.

key + board = *keyboard*   paint + brush = *paintbrush*

**Read each clue. The clue describes a compound word.
Then write the compound word on the line.**

1. Name an ache in your tooth.   _____

2. Name a field of corn.   _____

3. Name flakes of snow.   _____

4. Name a fish that looks like jelly.   _____

5. Name a storm of thunder.   _____

6. Name shelves for books.   _____

7. Name a boat driven by steam.   _____

**Circle the compound word in each phrase. Then draw a
line between the two parts of the compound word.**

8. through the waterway   9. in the summertime

10. dancing on a showboat   11. guided by torchlight

Through the Bayou by Torchlight by Currier & Ives

WORD STRATEGY

When you read,
divide an unfamiliar
compound word
into two smaller
words. This will
help you figure out
the pronunciation
and meaning of
the word. Use this
strategy to divide
these compound
words:

concertgoer
painstaking

⭐ **Here are two word lists. Draw a line to match a word from Column *A* with a word from Column *B*. Then write the five compound words on the lines.**

A	B
loud	case
bag	speaker
base	pipe
class	room
stair	ball

1. _____

2. _____

3. _____

4. _____

5. _____

⭐ **Read the compound words you wrote above. Write a sentence for each compound word.**

6. _____

_____

_____

7. _____

_____

_____

8. _____

_____

_____

9. _____

_____

_____

10. _____

_____

_____

 Home Involvement Activity Many compound words start or end with ball or light, as in ball**room**, foot**ball**, and light**house**. List other compound words that begin or end with these two smaller words.

Name _____

Some **compound words** have more than two syllables. Look at the compound word **watercolor.** How many syllables does it have? Here's how you can figure it out.

• First, break apart the compound word.
  watercolor = water + color

• Then count the number of syllables.
  Water has 2 syllables.
  Color has 2 syllables.
  2 + 2 = 4

The compound word **watercolor** has 4 syllables.

Separate each compound word into two smaller words. Write the two words. Count the number of syllables in each smaller word. Then add the number of syllables. The first one has been done for you.

Compound Word	Smaller Words		Syllables		
1. applesauce	apple	+ sauce	2	+ 1	= 3
2. watermelon	_____	+ _____	__	+ __	= __
3. motorcycle	_____	+ _____	__	+ __	= __
4. bookkeeper	_____	+ _____	__	+ __	= __
5. supermarket	_____	+ _____	__	+ __	= __
6. Thanksgiving	_____	+ _____	__	+ __	= __
7. ballplayer	_____	+ _____	__	+ __	= __
8. gentlemen	_____	+ _____	__	+ __	= __
9. paperweight	_____	+ _____	__	+ __	= __
10. handkerchief	_____	+ _____	__	+ __	= __

CHALLENGE

Separate each of these long compound words into two smaller words. Then write a sentence for each compound word.

newscaster
checkerboard
broncobuster

⭐ **Write** compound animal names. Draw a line to match a word from Column **A** with a word from Column **B**. Then write the name on the line. Draw a line up and down to separate each compound animal name into syllables.

A	B
star	tail
fire	pecker
grass	fish
wood	fly
cotton	worm
ant	hopper
bull	frog
inch	eater

1. _____

2. _____

3. _____

4. _____

5. _____

6. _____

7. _____

8. _____

⭐ **List** eight more compound animal names. Then separate each compound name into two smaller words. Count the number of syllables in each word. Finally, add the total number of syllables of all the words.

Compound Word	Smaller Words	Syllables
9. _____	_____ + _____	__ + __ = ___
10. _____	_____ + _____	__ + __ = ___
11. _____	_____ + _____	__ + __ = ___
12. _____	_____ + _____	__ + __ = ___
13. _____	_____ + _____	__ + __ = ___
14. _____	_____ + _____	__ + __ = ___
15. _____	_____ + _____	__ + __ = ___
16. _____	_____ + _____	__ + __ = ___

Total: _____

LESSON 45: Compound Words and Syllables

Home Involvement Activity Make a list of five imaginary compound animal names, such as a *brainbird* or a *turkeyworm*. Draw pictures of your animals. Label each picture with the funny compound animal name.

Name _____

★ **Read about a different kind of artist. Then answer the questions that follow.**

Twisted Trails

A nonfiction article from Time for Kids magazine

"Turtle" maze by Adrian Fisher, Edinburgh Zoo

Adrian Fisher is A-MAZE-ING! Mr. Fisher, who lives in England, designs mazes for a living. He makes walk-through mazes that people must solve by finding a clear path from entrance to exit.

A good maze requires careful planning and a real understanding of math. Adrian Fisher's job requires him to be part scientist and part artist. "I studied math in school, and I always loved gardening," he says. "Building mazes is a way to combine these two loves."

In 1996, Fisher broke a record by making the largest maze up to that time. This Michigan corn maze was in the shape of a car. At least 2,000 people could try to find their way through it at once.

Mr. Fisher takes pleasure in watching people walk through his mazes. "Eleven- and 12-year-old children are often better than their parents at making their way through mazes," Fisher says. "I especially like to watch adults go through them. They get lost right away, and it forces them to act like children for half an hour."

Do grown-ups take a professional puzzlemaker seriously? You bet. A museum in Florida has shown Fisher's mazes in a special show. That makes sense to Fisher. "Maze design is very much like art," says the maze master. "There's a story behind each one."

📖 Reader's Response

1. **What does Adrian Fisher do?**

2. **What might Adrian Fisher do first to design a maze? What might he do last?**

3. **Would you like to go through one of Adrian Fisher's mazes? Why or why not?**

Imagine having to walk through this maze. Where would you begin? Where would you end?

What would you do to get through this maze? Write a list of directions. Give your directions in order. Tell where you would walk first, next, and so on. Use at least four of these words.

first   next   then   finally   walk   through   path   obstacles   avoid

turn   right   left   straight   back   around   hedge   ahead   steps

_____

_____

_____

_____

_____

_____

_____

Writer's Tip

Use time-order words to give your directions. Tell what you would do *first*, *next*, *then*, and *finally* to walk through the maze.

Writer's Challenge

Write a list of directions to explain how you get to school. Use time-order words. Then draw a map to show the route you take.

LESSON 46: Connecting Reading and Writing
Comprehension—Sequence; Synthesize

Name _____

⭐ **Write the plural form of each of these base words. Make spelling changes as needed.**

1. tax _____
2. child _____
3. piano _____
4. waltz _____
5. mouse _____
6. deer _____
7. loaf _____
8. berry _____
9. monkey _____
10. man _____

⭐ **Rewrite each phrase. Use an apostrophe (') or an apostrophe and an s ('s) to show who or what has or owns something.**

11. the paints that belong to the artists _____

12. the game of the boy _____

13. the classroom of those teachers _____

14. the clay that belongs to the children _____

15. the blankets of those babies _____

16. the owners of the animals _____

⭐ **Read each sentence. Circle the word that correctly completes it. Then write the word on the line.**

17. *The Sound of Music* is _____ favorite movie.

    Moms   Mom's   Moms'

18. Many of this _____ songs are still popular.

    movie's   movies   movies'

19. Do you know the _____ to "My Favorite Things"?

    word's   words'   words

From the movie
The Sound of Music, 1965

Complete each sentence with a compound word.

1. Rooms for classes are _____.

2. A storm of thunder is a _____.

3. Fields where corn grows are _____.

4. A brush for painting is a _____.

Read the passage. Fill in the circle of the word that completes each numbered sentence.

Peter Tchaikovsky was one of **5** greatest composers. His best-known work is called *The Nutcracker Suite*. This is a **6** of musical pieces for a ballet. Dancers in colorful **7** act out scenes from a **8** dream. The "Dance of the Sugar Plum Fairy" is fun to hear. As the music plays, a ballerina on **9** dances as if she were on a cloud.

5. ○ Russia   ○ Russias   ○ Russia's

6. ○ series'   ○ series   ○ serie's

7. ○ outfits   ○ out fits   ○ outfits'

8. ○ childs   ○ child's   ○ children

9. ○ toetips   ○ tip toes   ○ tiptoes

Read the passage again to answer these questions. Circle the letter of your answer.

10. What was Tchaikovsky's country?
    a. America
    b. China
    c. Spain
    d. Russia

11. In music, what is a *suite*?
    a. a costume
    b. a set of musical pieces
    c. some bells
    d. a ballerina

Extend & Apply

Play the "Dance of the Sugar Plum Fairy" from *The Nutcracker Suite*. Close your eyes as you listen. What do you "see" in your mind? Tell about it in a short paragraph. Use at least one compound word.

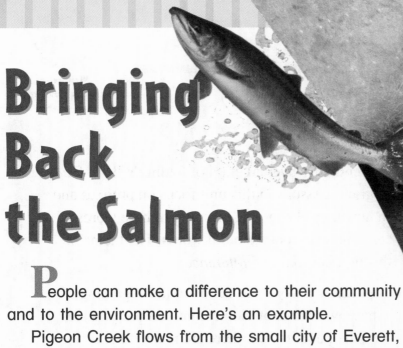

Bringing Back the Salmon

People can make a difference to their community and to the environment. Here's an example.

Pigeon Creek flows from the small city of Everett, Washington, into Puget Sound. In its last half-mile, the stream runs past Jackson Elementary School. Once, it was a clear stream, full of salmon. Fish were born there, grew there, and then swam to the sound and out to the Pacific Ocean. They always returned to their home stream to spawn. As the city grew around it, Pigeon Creek turned muddy. The salmon stayed away. Instead, all kinds of trash filled the stream. The water became polluted. The students at Jackson Elementary School decided to do something about the problem.

First, the students cleaned up the stream. They called on their neighbors to help. Then, the students cared for young salmon in tanks in their school. When the salmon were ready, the students released them into Pigeon Creek.

All the hard work paid off. Two years later, the salmon came back! The students had a right to be proud. They had solved a local problem and had really made a difference.

💡 Critical Thinking

1. How did Pigeon Creek become polluted?

2. What did the students do to solve the problem?

3. What can you learn from the Jackson Elementary School students?

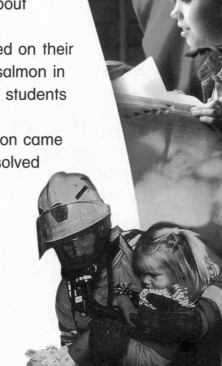

Internet

**Visit us at
www.sadlier-oxford.com**

UNIT 4
Making a Difference

Bringing Back the Salmon

People can make a difference to their community and to the environment. Here's an example.

Pigeon Creek flows from the small city of Everett, Washington, into Puget Sound. In its last half-mile, the stream runs past Jackson Elementary School. Once, it was a clear stream, full of salmon. Fish were born there, grew there, and then swam to the sound and out to the Pacific Ocean. They always returned to their home stream to spawn. As the city grew around it, Pigeon Creek turned muddy. The salmon stayed away. Instead, all kinds of trash filled the stream. The water became polluted. The students at Jackson Elementary School decided to do something about the problem.

First, the students cleaned up the stream. They called on their neighbors to help. Then, the students cared for young salmon in tanks in their school. When the salmon were ready, the students released them into Pigeon Creek.

All the hard work paid off. Two years later, the salmon came back! The students had a right to be proud. They had solved a local problem and had really made a difference.

Critical Thinking

1. How did Pigeon Creek become polluted?
2. What did the students do to solve the problem?
3. What can you learn from the Jackson Elementary School students?

Dear Family,

Your child has begun Unit 4 of Sadlier's *Word Study* program. Lessons in this unit focus on prefixes and on how they change the meaning of base words or combine with roots to build words. The theme of this unit is *making a difference*.

A **prefix** is a word part added to the beginning of a base word or root. Some common prefixes are **re-, dis-,** and **in-,** but there are many others.

A **base word** is any word to which a prefix may be added. For example, add the prefix **re-,** which means "again" or "back," to the base word **tell: re- + tell = retell.** The new word means "to tell again."

A **root** is the main part of a word. Roots, such as **-ject-,** often become words when prefixes are added to them:

re- + -ject- = reject.

LINKS TO LEARNING

To extend learning together, you might explore:

Web Sites
www.pmd.org

www.streamkeeper.org

Video
America's Endangered Species: Don't Say Good-bye, National Geographic Video.

Literature
Come Back, Salmon by Molly Cone, ©1992.

It's Our World, Too by Phillip Hoose, ©1993.

Kids With Courage: True Stories About Young People Making a Difference by Barbara A. Lewis, ©1992.

Family Focus

● Create a list or a Word Wall of the prefixes your child will study in this unit. Add words that use these prefixes whenever they arise— in conversation, on the radio or television, in the newspaper, or in the daily mail.

● Read together the article on page 99. Discuss it with your child. Does your community have any similar problems with pollution? What can your family do to help make a difference?

Name _____

Helpful Hints

A **prefix** is a word part added to the **beginning** of a **base word**.
Adding a prefix to a word can change the meaning of the word.
It can also make a new word.

The prefix **un** means "not," as in **un**afraid.
The prefix **dis** means "not" or "opposite of," as in **dis**like.
The prefix **re** means "again," as in **re**write, or "back," as in **re**turn.

Watch out for words that seem to have prefixes but really do not.
When you remove the **un** from **uncle,** no base word remains.

Add **un, re,** or **dis** to each of these base words. Write the new word on the line.

1. not **kind**

2. **pay** back

3. the opposite of **agree**

4. **fill** again

5. not **known**

6. not **important**

Read the base word at the left of each sentence. Add the prefix **un, re,** or **dis** to the base word. Write the new word on the line.

welcome 7. The members of the cleanup crew were

greeted by a(n) _____ sight.

safe 8. The amount of trash left over from the

parade made the street _____.

appear 9. The volunteers quickly went to work to make

the garbage _____.

store 10. They worked long and hard to _____ the street to its original condition.

pleasant 11. We are sorry their task was

so _____.

CHALLENGE

Some words have *two* prefixes. Underline the two prefixes in each of these words. Then tell what each word means.

unresolved

rediscovered

⭐ **Add the prefixes in red to the base words in the box. Write the new words on the lines.**

1 un	2 re	3 dis
familiar _____	place _____	connect _____
opened _____	turn _____	honest _____
able _____	view _____	color _____
happy _____	solve _____	loyal _____
checked _____	think _____	like _____
tie _____	live _____	approve _____

⭐ **Use the best word from above to complete each sentence correctly.**

4. Some people feel they are _____ to solve community problems.

5. If people are _____ with the problems in their community, they can do nothing to help solve them.

6. A community must _____ its problems by finding solutions.

7. If pollution goes _____, it can make people and animals sick.

8. Waste in rivers and streams can

   _____ the water, turning it from blue to muddy gray.

9. Yet rivers and streams can _____ to their original state with just a little help.

10. Scientists must _____ all the facts before choosing a plan of action.

11. Sometimes, scientists must _____ their solutions to problems.

12. Their solutions must not make people sad

    or _____.

LESSON 49: Prefixes **un-, re-, dis-**

Home Involvement Activity *Return of the Jedi* is a movie with a prefix in its title. Underline the prefix in the title of these videos your whole family can enjoy: *Egypt Uncovered* *Discovering Canada by Rail*

Name _____

Helpful Hints

The **prefix** pre means "before." To **pre**pay means "to pay before."

The **prefixes** in and im mean "not" or "into."

Inactive means "not active." **Im**press means "press into."

The **prefixes** over and super mean "beyond," "extra," or "too much."

To **over**eat means "to eat too much."

A **super**star is more talented than other stars.

Underline the prefix in each word. Then use what you know about the prefix to write the meaning of the word.

1. overjoyed _____

2. superhero _____

3. impatient _____

4. prehistoric _____

5. impressed _____

6. incredible _____

CHALLENGE

Pre- can be used to describe a period in time. Use a dictionary to write the meaning of these words:

Precambrian

pre-Columbian

Complete each sentence about Elizabeth Cady Stanton. Choose the best word from the activity above.

7. It seems _____ now, but before 1920, women in the United States were not allowed to vote.

8. Elizabeth Cady Stanton disagreed with that idea and _____ people with her speeches about women's rights.

9. Sometimes, she was _____ with the slow progress women were making.

10. She would be _____ to see the rights that women have gained today.

LESSON 50: Prefixes **pre-, in-, im-, over-, super-**   103

Choose a word from the box to answer each question correctly. Write the word on the line.

supermarket	impure	incorrect	overcast	imprison	inexact	superhero
overseas	indirect	overweight	immature	preview	overflow	

1. Which word means "not direct"? _____

2. Which word means "to view ahead of time"? _____

3. Which word means "not mature"? _____

4. Which word means "weighing too much"? _____

5. Which word means "a market greater than other food stores"? _____

6. Which word means "beyond the sea"? _____

7. Which word means "clouded over"? _____

8. Which word means "not correct"? _____

9. Which word means "to flow over"? _____

10. Which word means "a hero greater than other heroes"? _____

11. Which word means "not pure"? _____

12. Which word means "to put in prison"? _____

13. Which word means "not exact"? _____

Choose five words from the box above. Write a sentence for each word.

14. _____

15. _____

16. _____

17. _____

18. _____

LESSON 50: Prefixes **pre-, in-, im-, over-, super-**

Home Involvement Activity Write an index card for each of the five prefixes from this lesson. Then take turns picking a card. Say a word that starts with the prefix on the card you pick. Then use the word in a sentence.

Name _____

Read about a great musician who has spent a lifetime making a difference. Then answer the questions that follow.

A Musical Treasure

Isaac Stern was born in Russia in 1920. When he was ten months old, his family came to the United States. They settled in San Francisco. At the age of eight, Isaac began playing the violin. He has been playing ever since!

Isaac Stern is one of the world's "musical treasures." He is also a treasure for the kind of person he is. Stern has helped hundreds of students with their musical careers.

One of the highlights of Isaac Stern's career came in 1979. That year, he went to China. Few Americans could visit that country at that time. Yet Stern brought his violin with him as well as his desire to share his talent. This amazing trip was made into a movie. The movie is called *From Mao to Mozart: Isaac Stern in China*.

This wonderful film thrilled audiences. It even won an Academy Award. In the movie you can see Isaac Stern enjoying a concert of Chinese music. You can also see him explaining to Chinese music students that it is not enough just to play the right notes. True musicians must express their feelings as they play.

From Mao to Mozart shows Isaac Stern sharing his talent with young musicians. It also shows him using his music to change the world.

Reader's Response

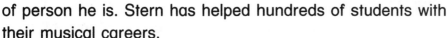

1. **Why is Isaac Stern famous?**

2. **Why might a famous person want to share his or her talent with young people?**

3. **Which of your talents could you share with someone? Explain.**

Isaac Stern visited China in 1979. There, he learned about Chinese music and culture. You, too, can learn about another culture—but without leaving home. How? You can become a pen pal.

Write a letter or send an e-mail to a pen pal. Your librarian or teacher can help you find a list of pen-pal names. Tell your pen pal about yourself, your family, your best friend, your school, and your community. Ask questions that you would like your pen pal to answer. Use at least two of these words.

hobbies	discover	unusual	important	typical	subjects
incredible	dislike	unfamiliar	background	culture	interests

Writer's Tip

Use clear details. Remember that a pen pal lives far away. He or she may not know the same things that you do.

Writer's Challenge

Write a letter persuading your family to let you visit your pen pal. Explain how your visit would make a difference not only to you and your pen pal but also to the world. Save your strongest reason for last.

LESSON 51: Connecting Reading and Writing
Comprehension—Make Inferences; Interpret

Name _____

Add the prefix un to two of the following base words. Add the prefix re to the two other words. Write the meaning of each new word.

Base Word	Word with Prefix	Meaning of New Word
1. afraid	_____	_____
2. turn	_____	_____
3. write	_____	_____
4. known	_____	_____

Add the prefix dis to two of the base words. Add the prefix pre to the two other words. Write the meaning of each new word.

Base Word	Word with Prefix	Meaning of New Word
5. agree	_____	_____
6. view	_____	_____
7. honest	_____	_____
8. historic	_____	_____

Add the prefix in to one of the base words. Add the prefix over to the other base word. Write the meaning of each new word.

Base Word	Word with Prefix	Meaning of New Word
9. direct	_____	_____
10. weight	_____	_____

Add the prefix im to one of the base words. Add the prefix super to the other base word. Write the meaning of each new word.

Base Word	Word with Prefix	Meaning of New Word
11. patient	_____	_____
12. market	_____	_____

Fill in the circle of the word that completes each sentence. Then write the word on the line.

1. Once you _____ how you can make a difference, lending a hand can be easy.
   ○ discover   ○ recover   ○ overcover

2. You don't have to be a _____ to help.
   ○ disloyal   ○ unknown   ○ superhero

3. A simple act of kindness can make you feel _____ proud.
   ○ incredibly   ○ incredible   ○ overjoyed

4. Most people will be _____ with how helpful you are.
   ○ impressed   ○ unpressed   ○ overpressed

Read this story about a helpful friend. Complete each sentence by combining the prefix with the base word in the box. Write the new word on the line.

Prefixes
un
re
in
over
Base Words
active
ate
tie
live

Amy (5)_____ at the pizza party. "Five pieces of pizza?" I exclaimed. Amy groaned and said she felt awful. I thought I might be able to

help. "Loosen your belt and (6)_____ your scarf," I said. "Now let's take a little walk. You'll feel better if you move around."

Amy wanted to stay (7)_____, but I insisted that she walk. We went out into the cool air. We slowly walked down the street. After a little while, Amy smiled weakly. "I'm still too full, but I feel a bit better. Thanks."

"Great!" I said. "Now let's go back inside and have some more lemonade."

"No!" Amy moaned. "I'm in no rush to

(8)_____ this feeling anytime soon!"

Extend & Apply

Write a paragraph about a time when you helped a friend, a relative, or a neighbor. Use at least two words with prefixes.

Name _____

Helpful Hints

Sub is a **prefix** meaning "under" or "less than."
A **sub**way runs under the street.

Co means "together" or "jointly."
A **co**pilot works with a pilot to fly an airplane.

Ex means "out of," "from," or "beyond."
I'd like to **ex**change this shirt for that one.

⭐ **Underline the prefix in each word.**

1. explain
2. subtopic
3. express
4. exclaim
5. cosign
6. suburban
7. coexist
8. subdivide
9. coauthor
10. subtitle
11. costar
12. submarine

⭐ **Unscramble the letters at the left to form a word that fits each clue. Write the word on the line. All the words appear in the list above.**

spxsere   13. to put into words   _____

tosrca   14. to star with someone else   _____

videudisb   15. to divide into more parts   _____

busicopt   16. a second, or less important, topic   _____

bmesnurai   17. a ship that can travel underwater   _____

rothcuao   18. to write a book together   _____

CHALLENGE

The words **un**like and **dis**like have different prefixes, but they share the same base word. Which prefixes that you have studied can you add to these base words?

_____press

_____solve

_____claim

Each box contains three prefixes and three base words.
Draw a line to connect a prefix with a base word.
Then write the new word on the line.

1		2		3	
ex	operate	co	standard	sub	sign
sub	plain	ex	educational	co	terminate
co	tropical	sub	claim	ex	merge
_____		_____		_____	
_____		_____		_____	
_____		_____		_____	

Complete each sentence below. Use a word from the boxes above.

4. To place underwater is to _____.

5. To _____ is to make clear or plain.

6. _____ places are hot and nearly tropical.

7. A _____ school is for both boys and girls.

8. Something that is below the standard is _____.

9. To _____ is to destroy or get rid of pests.

10. To _____ is to work together to get something done.

11. To cry or speak out is to _____.

12. To sign a document with other people is to _____.

The Declaration of Independence, July 4, 1776, by John Trumbull, c1800

LESSON 53: Prefixes **sub-, co-, ex-**

Home Involvement Activity What jobs can you name with the prefixes sub, co, or ex? How about a **sub**contractor, a **co**author, and an **ex**terminator? Make a list.

Name _____

Helpful Hints

The **prefixes il, ir, non,** and **mis** mean "not."

illegal = not legal   **ir**regular = not regular
nonstop = not stopping   **mis**trust = not trusting

The **prefix mis** can also mean "wrong" or "wrongly"
or "bad" or "badly."

misguided = wrongly guided
misconduct = bad conduct

Underline the prefix in each word.

1. mistake

2. irresistible

3. misspelled

4. nonsense

5. misuse

6. nonprofit

7. irresponsible

8. illogical

9. nonfiction

10. misplace

11. nonworking

12. illiterate

Answer each question. Use a word from the list above.

13. Which word means "not able to read
    or write"?   _____

14. Which word means "not responsible"?   _____

15. Which word means "to put in the
    wrong place"?   _____

16. Which word means "not making sense"? _____

17. Which word means "to use badly"?   _____

18. Which word means "wrongly spelled"?   _____

19. Which word means "not logical"?   _____

20. Which word means "not fiction"?   _____

WORD STRATEGY

To figure out the
meaning of an
unfamiliar word
with a prefix, cover
the prefix and read
the rest of the word.

Try that strategy
with these words.
Then write the
meaning of each
of the words.

mislead
nonviolent

LESSON 54: Prefixes **il-, ir-, non-, mis-**

Read each passage. The answer the question that follows it.

1. In Colonial times, the American colonists were taxed by the British. The colonists didn't approve. They felt that the British were not treating them well. What does it mean to be **mistreated**?

   _____

   _____

2. At first, the colonists didn't have a regular army. They formed groups of irregular soldiers to fight the British army. What is an **irregular** soldier?

   _____

   _____

3. Paul Revere was a real man who lived during the American Revolution. He fought for liberty. Revere's adventures read like a work of fiction. Yet they weren't fiction. What does **nonfiction** mean?

   _____

   _____

   _____

Painting of *The Midnight Ride of Paul Revere*

4. Thanks to the deeds of Paul Revere and other colonists, the patriots won the war. The patriots' decision to fight for independence was irreversible. One event led to the other, and there was no turning back. What does **irreversible** mean?

   _____

   _____

5. Many of the people who signed the Declaration of Independence had poor handwriting. Their names are hard to read. They are illegible. What does **illegible** mean?

   _____

   _____

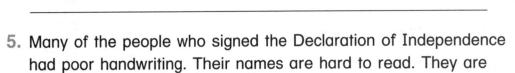

Home Involvement Activity Talk about the meaning of the words **legal** and **illegal**. Discuss why some things aren't legal. Then talk about the meanings of **responsible** and **irresponsible**. Come up with examples.

Name _____

Read about a brave woman who made a difference to our nation. Then answer the questions that follow.

Deciding What's Right

Daisy Bates was born and raised in a small town in Arkansas. She went to a school for black students only. White students went to other schools. Many people knew these separate schools were unequal. Daisy Bates was one of these people.

In 1954, the United States Supreme Court decided that it was unfair and illegal to allow separate schools for black and white students. However, many people in Arkansas and other Southern states disagreed. Despite the new law, many people refused to allow black children into white schools or white children into black schools. Some people, like Daisy Bates, wanted to test the new law. They did so by trying to register black children in white schools.

In 1957, Daisy Bates and her husband ran a newspaper. Through Daisy's words and acts, she succeeded in getting nine black students admitted to Central High School in Little Rock, Arkansas.

Daisy's efforts led to a big victory for civil rights. When she died in 1999, President Clinton called her a hero. Daisy *had* made a difference.

Reader's Response

1. Why weren't black students allowed to attend white schools in Arkansas in 1957? What do you think about this?

2. Do you agree that Daisy Bates was a hero? Explain your reasons.

3. What do you do when you feel something is unfair? Explain.

The true story of Daisy Bates shows that she was a hero. In fact, many people, including a President, admired her. Which person in your life do you admire? What are your reasons?

Write about someone special. Tell why you admire this person. Explain how this person has made a difference in your life or in the lives of other people. Use at least two of these words to describe your special person.

> unafraid   respect   superhero   discourage   impress   injustice
>
> overjoyed   mistake   cooperate   misunderstand   unfair   nonstop

Writer's Tip

Include strong details in your description so that your audience can see why this person is so special.

Speaker's Challenge

Work with a partner. Role-play an event that you wrote about in your description. Act out your event for the class. Use appropriate gestures. Will you play yourself or your special person? Why?

LESSON 55: Connecting Reading and Writing
Comprehension—Make Judgments and Decisions; Synthesize

Name _____

> ## Helpful Hints

The **prefix pro** means "forward," "before," "in favor of," or "for."

    promotion = moving someone forward in a job
    prologue = words before a poem or a play
    prodemocracy = in favor of democracy

The prefixes **com** and **con** mean "with" or "together."

    compile = to gather and put together
    confront = to bring face to face with

The prefix **under** means "below," "less than," or "not enough."

    underground = below the ground
    undercharge = to charge too little or not enough

Underline the prefix in each word. Then write the meaning of the word on the line.

1. pro-American _____

2. underage _____

3. confirm _____

4. undercover _____

5. prolong _____

6. underweight _____

7. composition _____

8. underpass _____

9. proclaim _____

10. underpaid _____

> ## CHALLENGE

The prefix **pro** can mean "for." What part of speech does a **pronoun** stand in *for*?

LESSON 56: Prefixes **pro-, com-, con-, under-**

115

⭐ **Use a word from the box for each clue. Write one letter in each space. Then read down the shaded column to answer the question below.**

> composition promote underage protest underhand underline compile
>
> profile underpass confirm undercooked underfoot proportion undershirt

1. another word for an essay ___ ___ ___ ___ ___ ___ ___ ___ ___ ___ ___

2. thrown with the hand kept below ___ ___ ___ ___ ___ ___ ___ ___ ___

3. to make firm or strengthen
   with the truth ___ ___ ___ ___ ___ ___ ___

4. a side view of the face ___ ___ ___ ___ ___ ___ ___

5. below the legal age ___ ___ ___ ___ ___ ___ ___ ___

6. not cooked enough ___ ___ ___ ___ ___ ___ ___ ___ ___ ___ ___

7. to be in the way ___ ___ ___ ___ ___ ___ ___ ___ ___

8. a shirt worn under a shirt ___ ___ ___ ___ ___ ___ ___ ___ ___

9. relation of one part to another ___ ___ ___ ___ ___ ___ ___ ___ ___ ___

10. to gather and put together ___ ___ ___ ___ ___ ___ ___

11. a passageway under a highway ___ ___ ___ ___ ___ ___ ___ ___ ___

12. to mark with a line under ___ ___ ___ ___ ___ ___ ___ ___ ___

13. to speak up for or against ___ ___ ___ ___ ___ ___ ___

14. to move to a higher job ___ ___ ___ ___ ___ ___ ___

From the movie
The Wizard of Oz, 1939

Question: In *The Wizard of Oz*, this kind of person is called a "good-deed doer." What is another word for someone who gives money to worthy causes?

Answer: _____

 Home Involvement Activity Pretend that your family has $1 million to donate to a few worthy causes. Which causes would you want to help? Why? How much would you give to each?

Name _____

Helpful Hints

The **prefix** uni means "one."	A **uni**cycle has only one wheel.
The **prefix** bi means "two."	A **bi**cycle has two wheels.
The **prefix** tri means "three."	A **tri**cycle has three wheels.

★ **Underline the prefix in each word in the box. Then use the words to complete the sentences. Use a word only once.**

> bicolored   tristate   unicorn   triangle   biweekly   uniform

1. Which word means "having two colors"? _____

2. What figure has three sides and three angles? _____

3. Which word means "twice a week"? _____

4. Which word describes something worn by members of a certain group? _____

5. Which word describes a make-believe animal with one horn on its forehead? _____

6. What is the word for a three-state area? _____

★ **Complete each sentence. Use a word from the box above.**

7. Our class chose a hospital in the _____ area.

8. On Mondays and Wednesdays, we made _____ visits to patients.

9. The _____ hospital rooms were blue and yellow.

10. Each room had a picture of a horselike _____.

11. The nurses' caps were shaped like a _____.

12. Each nurse's _____ was white.

CHALLENGE

Benjamin Franklin invented a pair of eyeglasses that helped him read a book and also see at a distance. Unscramble this word to "see" what Franklin invented:

facilbos

The **prefix** semi means "half," "partly," or "happening twice."

A **semi**circle is half a circle. **Semi**annually is twice a year.

The **prefix** mid means "in the middle of."

Midweek is the middle of the week.

Underline the prefix in each word in the box. Then use the words to complete the sentences. Use a word only once.

midair   semiannual   midnight   Midwestern   semifinal

semisweet   midway   semitropical   semiretired   midday

1. In some countries, people take a _____ nap.

2. Kansas City is a _____ city on the Missouri River.

3. The climate of southern Florida is _____.

4. Our family takes a _____ trip in the fall and the spring.

5. That horror movie will be on TV at _____.

6. New York City is _____ between Boston and Washington, DC.

7. The dog leaped up to catch the ball in _____.

8. I prefer milk chocolate, but my sister likes

the _____ kind.

9. Our team lost in the _____ game of the tournament.

10. Grandma is now

_____ and

works only part-time.

LESSON 57: Prefixes **uni-, bi-, tri-, mid-, semi-**

Home Involvement Activity The biathlon is a winter sporting event. The triathlon is a kind of outdoor race. Find out about these sports events. How does knowing about these races help you understand their names?

Name _____

Draw one line under the word that has a prefix in each phrase. Draw two lines under the prefix in the word.

1. has illegible handwriting
2. attends preschool each morning
3. circled in midair
4. an overnight guest
5. pilot of a biplane
6. costarring in a new movie
7. planted in a semicircle
8. returns for a visit
9. made an unfamiliar sound
10. rode in a submarine
11. exchanged dollars for *yen*
12. the Underground Railroad

Unscramble the letters at the left to form a word that fits each clue. Write the word on the line. All the words are from the box.

| bicuspid | overhead | rebuild | unlisted | dishonest |
| nonprofit | supermarket | misplace | semisweet | prehistoric |

vehodera 13. above your head _____

mauspretker 14. a large food store _____

dipuscib 15. a tooth with two points _____

emclispa 16. to put in the wrong place _____

ulidber 17. to build again _____

iperishtroc 18. before history _____

finptorno 19. not for profit _____

swtemsiee 20. only partly sweet _____

sidthones 21. not honest _____

dunsteil 22. not listed _____

WORK TOGETHER

Scramble the letters of five words with prefixes from this unit. Write each scrambled word on an index card. Then write a definition of the words on a separate index card. Have a partner unscramble each word and match it to its definition.

Underline the prefix in each word in the box. Then sort the words according to how many syllables they have. Write each word correctly in the chart below.

compass	subdivided	unpleasant	proclaim	midwinter
impossible	reunite	tricycle	overjoyed	cooperate
nonsense	explain	unicycle	incredible	preheat

1 Has Two Syllables	2 Has Three Syllables	3 Has Four Syllables
_____	_____	_____
_____	_____	_____
_____	_____	_____
_____	_____	_____
_____	_____	_____

Answer each question. Use a word from the chart above. Write the word on the line.

4. Which four-syllable word means "not possible"? _____

5. Which two-syllable word means "to make clear or plain"? _____

6. Which four-syllable word means "to work together"? _____

7. Which two-syllable word describes something that makes no sense? _____

8. Which three-syllable word describes a three-wheeled vehicle? _____

9. Which four-syllable word means "hard to believe"? _____

10. Which three-syllable word means "not pleasant"? _____

Home Involvement Activity Many vehicles include prefixes in their names. What are **tri**marans, **tri**remes, and super**tankers?** Find out together.

Name _____

Read each group of words. Say and spell each word in bold print. Repeat the word. Then sort the words. Write the words in the correct column below.

- painted her **profile**

- farm animals as a **subtopic**

- gave an **illogical** reason

- **coauthor** of the book

- in the **midday** sun

- a 10-speed **bicycle**

- drew a **semicircle**

- going **nonstop**

- kept **irregular** hours

- wearing a **uniform**

- **misunderstand** the point

- ride a **tricycle**

- use a **compass** for direction

- leave out the **unimportant** details

- **underline** the answer

- **exchange** a library book

Words with **Two Syllables**	Words with **Three Syllables**	Words with **Four Syllables**

SPELL & WRITE

How often do you go to the library? Libraries can make a big difference in how well you do in school. Thanks to Andrew Carnegie, more than 2,500 public libraries were built in the United States.

Carnegie was a poor boy when he came to the United States from Scotland. In time, he made a fortune in the steel business. Although Carnegie had very little schooling, he loved books. He gave money so that cities and towns could build their own libraries. Is there a Carnegie library in your town?

Andrew Carnegie (1835–1919)

In a paragraph, explain how public libraries can make a difference. Use two or more of these spelling words.

profile	subtopic	illogical	coauthor	midday	bicycle
semicircle	nonstop	irregular	uniform		misunderstand
tricycle	compass	unimportant	underline		exchange

_____

_____

_____

_____

_____

_____

_____

_____

Writer's Tip

Start with a clear main idea of your topic. Add strong supporting details.

Writer's Challenge

Use ideas from your paragraph to create a "library" poster for your school or community library. Write a slogan and illustrate it. Get across the idea that libraries can make a difference.

Name _____

Add the prefix sub to two of the following base words. Add the prefix ex to the two other words. Write the meaning of each new word.

Base Word	Word with Prefix	Meaning of New Word
1. urban	_____	_____
2. change	_____	_____
3. press	_____	_____
4. standard	_____	_____

Add the prefix ir to two of the base words. Add the prefix il to the two other words. Write the meaning of each new word.

Base Word	Word with Prefix	Meaning of New Word
5. regular	_____	_____
6. legal	_____	_____
7. responsible	_____	_____
8. legible	_____	_____

Add the prefix mis to one of the base words. Add the prefix pro to the other base word. Write the meaning of each new word.

Base Word	Word with Prefix	Meaning of New Word
9. place	_____	_____
10. long	_____	_____

Add the prefix under to one of the base words. Add the prefix bi to the other base word. Write the meaning of each new word.

Base Word	Word with Prefix	Meaning of New Word
11. cycle	_____	_____
12. ground	_____	_____

Read the sentences. Fill in the circle of the word that completes each sentence. Then write the word on the line.

1. In 1981, _____ in El Salvador got an idea to help people who were physically challenged.
   ○ coworkers   ○ preworkers   ○ biworkers

2. They opened a _____ pottery workshop called ACOGIPRI.
   ○ biprofit   ○ uniprofit   ○ nonprofit

3. ACOGIPRI helps make life better for people with _____.
   ○ exabilities   ○ disabilities   ○ unabilities

4. Members make things to sell over the Internet to people who

   _____ for the items.
   ○ repay   ○ tripay   ○ prepay

Complete each sentence by combining the prefix with the correct base word in the box. Write the new word on the line.

Prefixes
re
non
il
pro
Base Words
legal
claimed
turned
working

After eating breakfast at Dan's Diner, I **(5)**_____ there for lunch. The sign on the door said "NO DOGS ALLOWED." Yet I could see that a big brown dog was lying near my favorite booth. I thought it was

(6)_____ to let dogs into restaurants. So I asked Dan why someone would ignore the sign.

"Oh, that's Corky," Dan **(7)**_____. Her owner, Jake, is blind. Then I saw the dog's gentle face and the special leather harness that Corky wore. Dan said that the law permits service dogs to enter places where

(8)_____ dogs would be kept out. Maybe it would help if Dan changed the sign to say, "NO DOGS ALLOWED UNLESS WORKING."

Extend & Apply

A dog is a **quadruped**—it has four *(quadru)* feet *(ped)*. What would you call a person?

_____

Name _____

Helpful Hint

You can form a new word by adding a **prefix** to a **base word**.

un + **lucky** = unlucky = not lucky
re + **start** = restart = start again
re + **cycle** = recycle = cycle again

Read the clues. Combine the prefixes and the base words in the box to form words that will answer the clues. Write the new words on the lines. You can use a prefix and a base word more than once.

1. To knock over is to _____.

2. To come back is to _____.

3. To pay ahead of time is to _____.

4. To pay too much is to _____.

5. To heat ahead of time is to _____.

6. To heat too much is to _____.

7. To heat again is to _____.

8. Something not used is _____.

9. Something used too much is _____.

10. Something used too little is _____.

11. Something used again is _____.

12. To be the first to find out is to _____.

13. To get well again is to _____.

14. To be a spy is to work _____.

15. To pass through a cycle again is to _____.

Prefixes

un	pre
over	dis
under	re

Base Words

turn	pay
heat	cycle
used	cover

CHALLENGE

Not all words with a prefix have base words that can stand alone. Underline the words below that do have base words.

recycle
disturb
reject
undercurrent

Combine prefixes and base words to make as many words as you can. Write the words on the lines. If you are not sure about a word, look it up in the dictionary. Then use your words to answer the questions that follow.

Prefixes			
un	re	dis	under
pre	in	im	over
co	ex	il	ir
non	pro	semi	tri

Base Words			
circle	angle	cycle	claim
poisonous	charge	legal	star
cook	turn	possible	complete
view	write	responsible	kind

_____ _____ _____ _____

_____ _____ _____ _____

_____ _____ _____ _____

_____ _____ _____ _____

_____ _____ _____ _____

_____ _____ _____ _____

1. Which word means "not responsible"? _____

2. Which word means "not poisonous"? _____

3. Which word means "a half-circle"? _____

4. Which word means "not legal"? _____

5. Which word means "to write over" or "revise"? _____

6. Which word means "to star with another person"? _____

7. Which word means "to view ahead of time"? _____

8. Which word means "a figure with three sides and three angles"? _____

9. Which word means "not complete"? _____

10. Which word means "not kind"? _____

Home Involvement Activity Some words that are spelled the same have a different sound and a different meaning. **Invalid** and **invalid** are examples. How do you pronounce each word? What does each word mean?

Name _____

Helpful Hints

A **root** is the main part of a word. Roots have meaning, but few roots can stand alone. Roots often become words when **prefixes** or **suffixes** are added to them. When you know the meaning of a root, you can often figure out the meaning of a word.

Root	Word	Definition
pos means "put" or "place"	im**pos**e	= to place upon
pel means "push" or "drive"	ex**pel**	= to drive or push out
port means "carry"	im**port**	= to bring goods from one country into another
ject means "throw" or "force"	in**ject**	= to force into

Read each word in the box. Place it correctly in the chart.

expel	porter	posture	transport	reject	subject
report	expose	propellor	composition	repel	project

1 Words with **pos**	2 Words with **pel**	3 Words with **port**	4 Words with **ject**
_____	_____	_____	_____
_____	_____	_____	_____
_____	_____	_____	_____

Write the word from the chart that fits the definition.

5. to carry people or goods _____

6. to force out of school _____

7. to make known or reveal _____

8. to refuse to accept _____

WORK TOGETHER

With group members, browse through books or newspapers to find words formed from the roots in this lesson. List the words you find.

The **root** spect means "see," "look," or "examine."

To **in**spect is to look at carefully.

The **root** scrib or scrip means "write."

To scrib**ble** is to write carelessly.

Underline the root in each numbered word below. Then match the word with its meaning. Write the letter of the correct definition on the line.

____ 1. spectator   a. to look at something carefully

____ 2. describe   b. a doctor's written directions for using medicine

____ 3. spectacular   c. the writing for a play, film, or television show

____ 4. script   d. someone who watches something without taking part

____ 5. spectacles   e. a person who looks for gold, other metals, or oil

____ 6. inspect   f. to write, engrave, or print

____ 7. inscribe   g. to write or tell about in detail

____ 8. prospector   h. the colors of the rainbow

____ 9. prescription   i. eyeglasses

____ 10. spectrum   j. like a great show or display

Write the word from the box that completes each sentence.

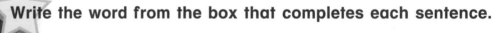

description   spectacle   inspector   prescribed   script

11. The witness gave a _____ of the earthquake.

12. The police _____ wrote everything down.

13. He wrote his notes in a very neat _____.

14. The doctor _____ medicine for the victims.

15. We looked out the window to view the _____.

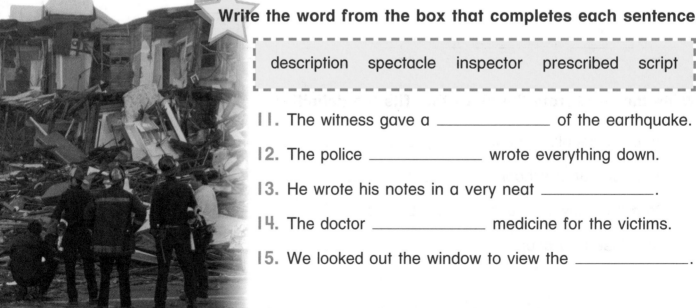

LESSON 62: Roots **-pos-, -pel-, -port-, -ject-, -spect-, -scrib-/-scrip-**

Home Involvement Activity Look for words that have the roots given in the lesson. You can find these words on signs, billboards, posters, ads, and Web sites. List the words you find.

Name _____

Helpful Hints

Here are more **roots** that appear in many English words. The **root duc** means "lead" or "bring."

re**duc**e = to bring down in size or amount

con**duc**t = to lead

The **root tract** means "pull," "drag," or "draw away."

tractor = a vehicle used for pulling farm machinery

Read each definition. Then find the verb in the box that matches it. Write the word on the line. Circle its root.

conduct	attract	reduce	subtract
extract	produce	distract	educate

1. to draw someone's attention away from something _____

2. to lead an orchestra _____

3. to take away one number from another _____

4. to create or bring forth _____

5. to pull toward oneself _____

6. to pull out a tooth _____

7. to bring down in size or amount _____

8. to lead to knowledge _____

Choose three words from above. Write a sentence for each word.

9. _____

10. _____

11. _____

CHALLENGE

The Latin roots **duc** and **tract** mean "bring" and "pull." Use what you know about prefixes and these roots to write a sentence for each of these verbs:

induct

retract

Use a word from the box to solve each clue. Write one letter in each space. Then copy all the letters that appear in the shaded boxes. Unscramble these letters to answer the question at the bottom of the page.

attract   retracts   deposit   distract   inspect

inscribe   spectator   produce   propel   respects

1. looks at someone with high regard
__ __ __ __ __ ☐ __ __ __

2. to pull toward oneself
__ __ __ ☐ __ __ __

3. to create or bring forth
__ ☐ __ __ __ __ __

4. to draw someone's attention away from something
__ __ __ ☐ __ __ __ __

5. to push or drive forward
__ __ ☐ __ __ __

6. to write, engrave, or print
__ ☐ __ __ __ __ __ __

7. pulls back or withdraws
__ __ __ __ ☐ __ __

8. to place or lay down
__ __ __ ☐ __ __ __

9. to look at something carefully
__ __ __ __ __ ☐ __

10. someone who watches something without taking part
__ __ __ __ ☐ __ __ __ __

Scrambled letters from boxes: _____

Simon volunteers his time for a good cause. He helps a group to build houses for the homeless. He plans and organizes the building. He makes sure that people have the tools they need and that each task gets done.

Question: What is the name of Simon's job?

Answer: _____

Home Involvement Activity The word **produce** has different pronunciations and different meanings, depending on which syllable you accent. Pronounce this word and discuss its different meanings.

Name _____

Read each word. Draw one line under the prefix. Draw two lines under the root. Then write the number of syllables in the word.

Word	Syllables	Word	Syllables
1. report	_____	2. propellor	_____
3. subject	_____	4. subtraction	_____
5. inspection	_____	6. conductor	_____
7. producer	_____	8. disposal	_____
9. composition	_____	10. reject	_____
11. contract	_____	12. injection	_____
13. prescription	_____	14. subscribe	_____
15. propose	_____	16. export	_____

Form a new word by putting together the prefix or prefixes and root. Write the new word. Then write the number of syllables that the word has.

	Word	Syllables
17. pro + duct	_____	_____
18. super + scribe	_____	_____
19. over + pro + duce	_____	_____
20. dis + re + spect	_____	_____
21. under + re + port	_____	_____
22. super + im + pose	_____	_____

> **CHALLENGE**
>
> Circle the prefixes in the words below. Underline the roots. How many syllables does each word have? What does each word mean?
>
> underproduce
> oversubscribe

⭐ **Each phrase below has a word with one or more prefixes. Underline the word. Then write it on the line. Divide the word into syllables by using a hyphen (-).**

1. produce good work _____

2. more exports to China _____

3. prescribes bed rest _____

4. a good subject _____

5. shows disrespect _____

6. needs to reduce class size _____

7. reimpose a tax _____

8. dispose of the trash _____

9. knows when to add and subtract _____

10. reinspect the boxes _____

⭐ **Use the words with prefixes above to answer the questions.**

11. Which two-syllable word means "goods carried or sent to other countries"? _____

12. Which two-syllable word means "to put out of the way" or "get rid of"? _____

13. Which two-syllable word means "to take away one number from another"? _____

14. Which three-syllable word means "to place upon again"?

_____

15. Which three-syllable word means "to look at carefully again"?

_____

LESSON 64: Syllables with Prefixes and Roots

Home Involvement Activity For three minutes, listen for long words on radio or television. Jot down the words. Figure out how many syllables each word has. Then check the word with the greatest number of syllables.

Name _____

READ & WRITE

⭐ **Read about a student, Dwaina Brooks, who has made a difference in the lives of the homeless. Then answer the questions that follow.**

It's Our World, Too!
Stories of Young People Who Are Making a Difference
by Phillip Hoose

Each morning on her way to school, Dwaina Brooks saw the line of men and women outside a homeless shelter and soup kitchen in Dallas. At school, her fourth-grade class was doing a unit on homelessness. Once a week, students telephoned a shelter and talked with someone who was staying there. Dwaina would ask the person on the other end of the phone. "What do you need?" The answer was always "a home" or "a job." It never seemed as though she could do much. Then one afternoon, Dwaina talked with a young man who had been without a home for a long time.

"What do you need?" she asked him.

"I would love a really good meal again."

"Well, now," said Dwaina, brightening. "I *can* cook."

Dwaina tore into the house that night after school and found her mother, Gail. As usual, she was in the kitchen. "Mama," she said. "I need you to help me fix some stuff to take down to that shelter we call at school. Let's make up as much as we can. Sandwiches and chicken. Let's get everyone to do it. C'mon."

In a little more than two years, Dwaina has organized several thousand meals for unfortunate people in the Dallas area. She and her mother and the classmates who sometimes still join in have perfected the art of helping others and having fun at the same time.

📖 Reader's Response

1. **What is the main idea of this true story?**

2. **What details show you that Dwaina has made a difference?**

3. **If you could meet Dwaina, what would you ask her? Why?**

Dwaina Brooks has helped change the lives of thousands of homeless people. One way she did this was to make meals for the homeless. Another way was to explain to students and adults how they, too, could make a difference.

Think of something you have done that has made a difference to a person, an animal, or your community. Explain in a paragraph what you did, why you did it, and how it helped. Be sure to speak in your own voice. Use at least two of these words.

produce	important	impossible	overlook	understand	positive
report	position	object	subject	respect	attract

_____

_____

_____

_____

_____

_____

_____

_____

_____

_____

Writer's Tips

Summarize your ideas at the end of your writing. Combine any sentences that you can. Remember to leave your audience with something to think about.

Speaker's Challenge

Give your paragraph as a speech to your class. Begin with your purpose. Speak loudly and clearly so that everyone can hear you. Make eye contact to keep your audience's interest. Leave time for questions and answers at the end of your speech.

Name _____

⭐ **Look at the word-part chart below. You can use it to form many words. For example, you can form the word respect by combining B1 + G2.**

	1	2	3
A	un	duc	able
B	re	tract	er
C	dis	port	tion
D	pre	pos	ing
E	in	ject	al
F	im	pel	ed
G	ex	spect	or
H	pro	scrib	less
I	sub	scrip	ment

⭐ **Use the word-part chart to decode these words. On the lines, write the words you get from these letters and numbers.**

1. I1 + B2 _____

2. E1 + G2 _____

3. G1 + F2 _____

4. B2 + G3 _____

5. I1 + I2 + C3 _____

6. C1 + B2 _____

7. B1 + C2 + B3 _____

8. H1 + E2 _____

9. H1 + D2 + E3 _____

10. B1 + A2 + C3 _____

11. B1 + E2 + F3 _____

12. D1 + I2 + C3 _____

⭐ **Use the word-part chart to encode these words. Write the letters and the numbers on the lines.**

13. export _____

14. production _____

15. subject _____

16. disposable _____

17. importing _____

18. inscription _____

Read the passage. For each numbered blank, there is a choice of words below. Fill in the circle of the word that correctly completes the sentence. Then write the word on the line.

Oseola McCarty grew up poor. She quit school after the sixth grade to care for a sick aunt. She earned money by washing and ironing other people's clothes. It was dull work.

Yet she did it without **(1)**_____.

When she was 87, Oseola went to visit the University of Southern Mississippi. She could not have gone there as a girl. African Americans could not go there then. Oseola gave the college $150,000 to help poor students. "I'm too old to get an education, but they can," she said.

How did Oseola get so much money? She **(2)**_____ for the future. She made weekly **(3)**_____ into her bank account.

Oseola might have been **(4)**_____ to most people. However, by the time she died at age 91, the world knew she had made a difference.

1. ○ compliment   ○ complaint   ○ comma

2. ○ prepared   ○ repaired   ○ retired

3. ○ details   ○ delays   ○ deposits

4. ○ unbroken   ○ unknown   ○ uneasy

Read the passage again to answer these questions. Circle the letter of the correct answer.

5. How did Oseola McCarty make a living?
   a. She was a teacher.
   b. She worked in a bank.
   c. She did people's laundry.
   d. She worked at a college.

6. Why did she give money to the university?
   a. She had once been a student there.
   b. She wanted to help others.
   c. She disliked having so much money.
   d. She was retired.

Extend & Apply

Oseola saved money for the future. What will you save money for someday?

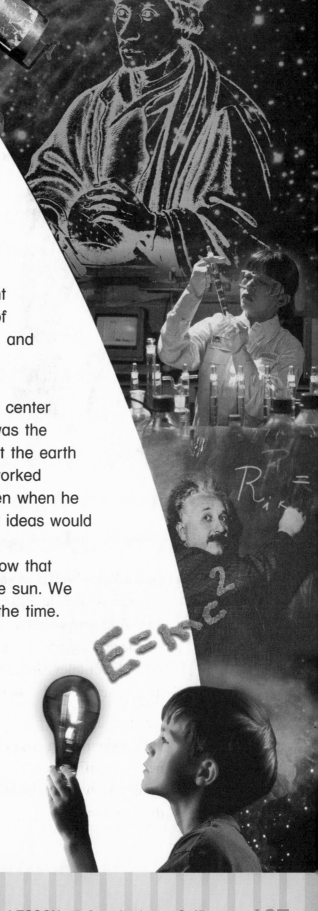

The Sky Is the Limit

Look up at the night sky on a clear evening. If you know where to look, you will see planets like Venus and Jupiter. Look again later, and you will see that these planets have moved.

For many years, people saw that stars and planets were in different parts of the sky at different times. They thought that the earth was the center of the universe. They believed that the moon, the sun, and all the planets moved around the earth.

Then along came Nicolaus Copernicus, a Polish astronomer. He did not think that the earth was the center of the universe. Instead, he believed that the sun was the center of the Solar System. Copernicus thought that the earth and the other planets rotated around the sun. He worked carefully to prove that his idea was correct. Yet even when he had it all figured out, Copernicus knew that his new ideas would make some people angry.

We know now that Copernicus was right. We know that the planets in our Solar System all move around the sun. We also know that scientists are proving new ideas all the time.

Critical Thinking

1. **What did Copernicus believe?**

2. **Why did he think his idea would make some people angry?**

3. **Would you be angry at someone for having an idea that was different from your own? Give reasons for your answer.**

The Sky Is the Limit

Look up at the night sky on a clear evening. If you know where to look, you will see planets like Venus and Jupiter. Look again later, and you will see that these planets have moved.

For many years, people saw that stars and planets were in different parts of the sky at different times. They thought that the earth was the center of the universe. They believed that the moon, the sun, and all the planets moved around the earth.

Then along came Nicolaus Copernicus, a Polish astronomer. He did not think that the earth was the center of the universe. Instead, he believed that the sun was the center of the Solar System. Copernicus thought that the earth and the other planets rotated around the sun. He worked carefully to prove that his idea was correct. Yet even when he had it all figured out, Copernicus knew that his new ideas would make some people angry.

We know now that Copernicus was right. We know that the planets in our Solar System all move around the sun. We also know that scientists are proving new ideas all the time.

Critical Thinking
1. What did Copernicus believe?
2. Why did he think his idea would make some people angry?
3. Would you be angry at someone for having an idea that was different from your own? Give reasons for your answer.

LESSON 67: Introduction to Suffixes and Syllables   137

Dear Family,

Your child has begun Unit 5 of Sadlier's *Word Study* program. Lessons in this unit focus on common suffixes and on how they affect the base words they follow. The theme of this unit is *scientists*.

A **suffix** is a word part added to the end of a word. Suffixes change the meanings of words or make new words. Some common suffixes are **-ful, -ness, -ly, -able, -ity,** and **-less.**

A **syllable** is a word or part of a word that makes a single sound. If a suffix contains a vowel sound, it is a syllable. To separate words with suffixes into syllables, divide between the base word and the suffix.

Family Focus

- Post a Word Wall of words that end with the suffixes your child will be studying in this unit. Add new words to the list of suffixes whenever they arise—in conversation, on the radio or television, in newspapers or magazines, or in the daily mail.

- Read together the passage on page 137. Talk about it with your child. Discuss a new scientific discovery that affects your family. How will it change the way you think or live?

LINKS TO LEARNING

Web Sites
www.antwrp.gsfc.nasa.gov/apod/astropix.html
www.iln.net/main/astronomy/planets.asp

Videos
Space Explorers, NOVA, PBS Home Video.

Planet Earth, Emmy Award Winner, Discovery Channel Video.

Literature
Space by Alan Dyer and Cliff Watts, © 1999.

The Young Astronomer by Harry Ford, © 1998.

Name _____

Helpful Hints

A **suffix** is a word part added to the end
of a **base word**. Suffixes change the meanings
of words or make new words.

round + **ness** = round**ness**   wild + **ly** = wild**ly**

• Add the suffix **er** to compare *two* things.
  fresh + **er** = fresh**er**

• Add the suffix **est** to compare *more than two* things.
  green + **est** = green**est**

Sometimes, you need to make spelling changes before
adding **er** or **est**.

• Double the **consonant** before adding **er** when a word
  ends in a consonant after a short vowel.
  ho**t** + **er** = ho**tter**

• Change **y** to **i** before adding **er**.
  happ**y** + **er** = happ**ier**

• Drop **silent** e before adding **est**.
  pal**e** + **est** = pal**est**

• Change **y** to **i** before adding **est**.
  wav**y** + **est** = wav**iest**

The planet Venus

⭐ **Add er and est to each base word. Write the new words
in the chart. Make needed spelling changes.**

	Base Word	Base Word + er	Base Word + est
1	smooth		
2	sturdy		
3	red		
4	fine		
5	flat		
6	easy		

WORK TOGETHER

Choose a partner.
Discover some
facts about planets.
Add the suffix **er** or
est to base words
such as **near,
close, heavy,
large,** and **small,**
to compare facts
about planets.

Read each sentence. Draw one line under the word that compares two things. Draw two lines under the word that compares more than two things.

1. A modern telescope is a finer instrument than a spyglass.

2. Copernicus' telescope was clumsier than the telescope used by Galileo.

3. The world's largest telescope is the Keck in Hawaii.

4. The Keck is sharper than an ordinary telescope.

5. The Keck's mirrors are the biggest of all the earth's telescopes.

6. The astronauts who repaired the Hubble Space Telescope had the hardest job of all the astronauts.

7. Of all telescopes, the Hubble is the farthest from the earth.

8. The Hubble's view of the earth is the greatest of all telescopes.

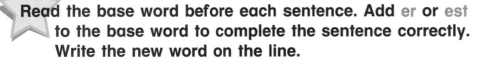

The Hubble Space Telescope

Read the base word before each sentence. Add er or est to the base word to complete the sentence correctly. Write the new word on the line.

strong   9. The telescope built by Galileo was _____ than the telescope used by Copernicus.

dark   10. Usually, the _____ the sky, the better the view with a telescope.

early   11. Observatories on mountains or on towers were the _____ ones built.

old   12. The _____ observatory still in use today is in Paris.

dense   13. Venus has a _____ atmosphere than Earth has.

cloudy   14. Even on the _____ nights, radio telescopes with computers can work.

wide   15. Puerto Rico's large Arecibo radio receiver is much _____ than a football field.

Home Involvement Activity Discuss these questions: Which day of the year is the longest? The shortest? Why? What are these two special days called?

Name _____

The **suffix** ful means "full of."

   Joyful means "full of joy."
   Beautiful means "full of beauty."

The **suffix** ment means "result of," "act of," or "state of being."

   Improvement is the result of being improved.
   Movement is the act of moving.
   Disappointment is the state of being disappointed.

The **suffix** ness means "a state of being."

   Greatness is the state of being great.

CHALLENGE

Make three lists. Use these headings: **ful**, **ment**, and **ness**. Write at least three words that use each of those suffixes.

Underline the suffix in each word.

1. measurement   2. payment   3. vastness

4. argument   5. powerful   6. wonderful

7. delightful   8. careful   9. awareness

10. helpful   11. contentment 12. enjoyment

Answer each question. Use the words from the list above.

13. Which word means "full of delight"?   _____

14. Which word means "the result of being paid"? _____

15. Which word means "the act of measuring"?   _____

16. Which word means "being aware"?   _____

17. Which word means "full of power"?   _____

18. Which word means "being contented"?   _____

19. Which word means "full of care"?   _____

The **suffix** ly means "how" or "in a certain way."

    Neatly means "in a neat way."

• When you add ly to a word that ends in le, drop the le.

   humble + ly = humbly   possible + ly = possibly

• When a word ends in y, change the y to i before adding ly.

   happy + ly = happily   mighty + ly = mightily

The **suffix** y means "full of" or "having."

    Lucky means "having luck."

• When a word ends in **silent** e, usually drop the e before adding y.

   bone + y = bony   mange + y = mangy

• When a word ends in a single consonant after a short vowel, double the consonant before adding y.

   skin + y = skinny   fun + y = funny

Read each phrase. Add y or ly to the word in bold print. Write the new word on the line.

1. in a **quick** way   _____

2. in an **easy** way   _____

3. full of **leaks**   _____

4. having **salt**   _____

5. full of **fun**   _____

6. in a **safe** way   _____

7. full of **noise**   _____

8. in a **serious** way _____

9. full of **bounce**   _____

10. in a **sad** way   _____

11. full of **bubbles**   _____

LESSON 69: Suffixes **-ful, -ment, -ness, -ly, -y**

Home Involvement Activity Write the five suffixes, ful, ment, ness, ly, and y, each on an index card. Shuffle the cards. For each card you pick, say a word that uses the suffix. Then use the word in a sentence about science.

Name _____

The **suffix** like means "resembling."
   Desertlike means "resembling a desert."
The **suffix** able means "can be."
   Washable means "can be washed."
The **suffix** age means "act or result of," "collection of," or "condition of."
   break**age**   lugg**age**   wreck**age**
If a word ends in **silent** e, drop the e before adding age.
   stor**age**
The **suffix** age can also mean "cost of," "home of," or "amount of."
   post**age**   orphan**age**   mile**age**
- When a word ends in **y** after a **consonant,** change the y to i
  before adding a suffix that does not begin with i.
     car**ry** + **age** = carr**iage**   mar**ry** + **age** = marr**iage**
- When a suffix that begins with a vowel follows a one-syllable,
  short-vowel word ending in a consonant, double the consonant
  before adding the suffix.
     b**a**g + **age** = ba**gg**age

⭐ **Underline the suffix in each word in bold print.**

1. a **lifelike** statue
2. film **footage**
3. a **springlike** day

4. fifty cents in **postage**
5. **remarkable** luck
6. **unbearable** heat

7. placed in the **carriage**
8. a **profitable** business
9. a secret **passage**

⭐ **Fill in the circle of the suffix that can be added to each base word. Write the new word on the line.**

10. comfort   ◯ able   ◯ age _____

11. business   ◯ like   ◯ age _____

12. orphan   ◯ age   ◯ able _____

13. accept   ◯ age   ◯ able _____

CHALLENGE

Unscramble the word in red. Then underline its suffix.

This jacket is leabviala in four different colors.

Now write another sentence using the unscrambled word.

Each box below contains three base words and three suffixes. Draw a line to connect each base word with a suffix to form three words. Then write the words on the lines.

1			2			3		
short	like		lug	able		remark	like	
profit	age		enjoy	like		post	age	
web	able		desert	age		child	age	

_____   _____   _____

_____   _____   _____

_____   _____   _____

Complete each sentence about a "dig" for dinosaur bones. Write the best word from the boxes above.

4. The scientists hoped their stay in this dry place would be _____.

5. They knew that the dry, _____ landscape would be filled with dinosaur bones.

6. Unfortunately, they had to live with a _____ of food and water.

7. Their _____ had little room for clothing in order to make space for tools and equipment.

8. The scientists paid extra _____ to have samples sent back to the laboratory.

9. One day, they made a _____ discovery—a complete skeleton of a dinosaur!

10. At first, they noticed the skeleton's thick,

    _____ toes.

11. A video camera captured

    the scientists' _____ glee when they made their discovery.

LESSON 70: Suffixes -like, -able, -age

Home Involvement Activity Make a list of the suffixes taught so far. Then have your child go through a page of his or her social studies, science, or reading book to write words that use the suffixes on the list.

Name _____

Helpful Hints

A **syllable** is a word or part of a word that makes a single sound. If a **suffix** contains a vowel sound, it is a syllable. To separate words with suffixes into syllables, divide between the base word and the suffix.

| tall-er | light-est | help-ful | short-age |

★ Each phrase below has a word with a suffix. Underline the word. Then write it on the line. Divide the word into syllables by using a hyphen (-).

1. fell on the pavement _____

2. a graceful swan _____

3. a shortage of food _____

4. the brightness of the sun _____

5. sees movement on the horizon _____

6. a salty taste in my mouth _____

7. moves as speedily as a shark _____

8. the deepest part of the ocean _____

WORD STRATEGY

Don't let a long word throw you. Take it apart. Look for prefixes, suffixes, and the base word to understand the word's meaning.

Now try the strategy. Draw one line under the prefix and two lines under the suffix in the two words below. Then write a sentence for each word.

disagreement
unforgettable

★ Use a word from the box below to answer each question. Write the word on the line.

| nicely | catlike | amazement | lovable | delightful |

9. Which two-syllable word means "resembling a cat"? _____

10. Which three-syllable word means "full of delight"? _____

11. Which three-syllable word means "being amazed"? _____

12. Which three-syllable word means "can be loved"? _____

13. Which two-syllable word means "in a nice way"? _____

Read each word. Underline the suffix. Then on the line, write the number of syllables that the word has.

Word	Syllables	Word	Syllables
1. funnier	_____	2. available	_____
3. smoothest	_____	4. birdlike	_____
5. careful	_____	6. tenderness	_____
7. smarter	_____	8. wildest	_____
9. agreeable	_____	10. younger	_____
11. seriously	_____	12. domelike	_____
13. thirstiest	_____	14. enjoyable	_____
15. breakable	_____	16. completely	_____
17. shipment	_____	18. darkness	_____
19. windy	_____	20. colorful	_____
21. profitable	_____	22. prettily	_____
23. yardage	_____	24. shortness	_____
25. argument	_____	26. development	_____
27. usage	_____	28. kindness	_____

Choose six of the words from above. Write a sentence for each word.

29. _____

30. _____

31. _____

32. _____

33. _____

34. _____

LESSON 71: Suffixes and Syllables

Home Involvement Activity Wattage is a measure of electric power expressed in watts. It is named after the inventor James Watt. Make a list of other words you can think of that are named after inventors or scientists.

Name _____

Helpful Hints

The **suffix ity** means "state or condition."

humid + ity = humidity
Humidity means "the state of being humid."

The **suffix ive** means "able to" or "tending."

invent + ive = inventive
Inventive means " able to invent."

The **suffixes ion, sion,** and **tion** mean "the act, state, or result of."

complete + ion = completion
Completion is the act of completing.

Galileo explaining his telescope to the English poet, John Milton

Underline the suffix in each word. Then use the word to write a sentence on the line.

1. active _____

2. electricity _____

3. rotation _____

4. creative _____

5. authority _____

Use a word from the box below to complete each sentence correctly.

> conclusions   fascination   attention

6. Copernicus was not the only scientist to have a

_____ with the universe.

7. Galileo also turned his _____ to the night sky.

8. He soon came to the same _____ about the universe that Copernicus had.

CHALLENGE

Sometimes, the spelling of a word changes when the suffix **ion, sion,** or **tion** is added.

divide = division

Underline the spelling changes in these words:

collide = collision
decide = decision

Explain the spelling changes to a classmate.

Sometimes, when a word ends in **silent** e, drop the e and add ion.

tense + ion = tension   confuse + ion = confusion

Write a word from the box to answer each question.

| operation | election | discussion | decision |
| subtraction | education | protection | pollution |

1. Which word means "the act of operating"?   _____

2. Which word means "the act of discussing"?   _____

3. Which word means "the act of educating"?   _____

4. Which word means "the result of polluting"?   _____

5. Which word means "the act of subtracting"?   _____

6. Which word means "the act of protecting"?   _____

7. Which word means "the result of electing"?   _____

8. Which word means "the act of deciding"?   _____

**Fill in the circle of the word that completes each sentence.
Then write the word on the line.**

9. Galileo's ideas got a _____ reaction from many people.
   ○ decision   ○ negative   ○ tension

10. One of Galileo's most important _____ to science was
    the scientific method.
         ○ education   ○ contributions   ○ protections

11. Isaac Newton's ideas about gravity also took science in the

    right _____.
         ○ direction   ○ discussion   ○ collision

12. Albert Einstein's theory of _____ changed the way we
    think about space and time.
         ○ relativity   ○ reactions   ○ relatives

Home Involvement Activity Work together to create
one long sentence about planets and stars. Include as
many suffixes from this lesson as you can.

LESSON 72: Suffixes **-ity, -ive, -ion,
          -sion, -tion**

Name _____

Read each group of words. Say and spell each word in bold print. Repeat the word. Then sort the words according to the number of syllables that the words have. Write the words in the correct column below.

- an **earlier** time
- **possibly** the oldest
- took it **seriously**
- **vastness** of the universe
- the **development** of radar
- **attention** to detail
- an **authority** on space travel
- write your **conclusion**
- unpack her **luggage**
- **domelike** buildings
- a **creative** mind
- **observation** deck

- the **rotation** of the earth
- a **graceful** dancer
- the **noisy** storm
- a **remarkable** shower of stars

McDonald Observatory in Texas

Words with **Two Syllables**	Words with **Three Syllables**	Words with **Four Syllables**

Since the beginning of time, people have made up stories about the night sky and about the changes in nature. For example, people imagined that they saw pictures in the stars. These pictures led storytellers to make up myths about the stars and constellations. People also made up stories about why thunder and lightning exist. Today, we have scientific facts to explain these natural events. Yet the old myths still entertain us.

Make up a myth that tells *why* something happens in nature. For example, you might explain why volcanoes erupt, or why Sirius (the Dog Star) is the brightest star in the sky. Use two or more of these spelling words in your myth.

earlier   possibly   seriously   vastness   development

attention   authority   conclusion   luggage   domelike   creative

observation   rotation   graceful   noisy   remarkable

Writer's Tips

Get ideas for your myth by reading some "how" or "why" stories. You can also get ideas from the animal names and shapes of constellations. Write a strong beginning, middle, and end.

Writer's Challenge

Observe the stars on a clear night. Take a flashlight, a notebook, and a pencil with you. Describe what you see. Be creative! Then write a poem about the stars.

Name _____

⭐ **Add** the sufffix er to two of the following base words. Add the suffix est to the other two. Tell what each new word means.

Base Word	Word with Suffix	Meaning of New Word
1. happy	_____	_____
2. funny	_____	_____
3. fine	_____	_____
4. hot	_____	_____

⭐ **Add** the suffix ful to two of the following base words. Add the suffix ly to the other two. Tell what each new word means.

Base Word	Word with Suffix	Meaning of New Word
5. help	_____	_____
6. possible	_____	_____
7. power	_____	_____
8. easy	_____	_____

⭐ **Add** the suffix age to one of the following base words. Add the suffix able to the other one. Tell what each new word means.

Base Word	Word with Suffix	Meaning of New Word
9. comfort	_____	_____
10. bag	_____	_____

⭐ **Add** the suffix ity to one of the following base words. Add the suffix ion to the other one. Tell what each new word means.

Base Word	Word with Suffix	Meaning of New Word
11. electric	_____	_____
12. invent	_____	_____

Read the sentences. Choose the word from the box that completes each sentence correctly. Write the word on the line.

inventive	safely	beautiful	development	unbearable

Jacques Cousteau

1. It is _____ to have to hold your breath for more than a few minutes.

2. Then how could people ever study the _____ ocean floor?

3. Jacques Cousteau was an _____ young sailor.

4. His _____ of air tanks came in 1943.

5. Cousteau wore the tanks on his back, while hoses brought air _____ to his mouth.

Read this true story about a scientist. Choose the word from the box that completes the sentence correctly. Write the word on the line.

education	seriously	creative	discussion

People once said that women couldn't be scientists.

Women who had an interest in science were not taken

(6)_____. Yet Dr. Cornelia Clapp studied animal

life more than a century ago. She also taught at a college

for women. Dr. Clapp believed that hands-on laboratory work

was important to a good science (7)_____.

Back then, there were few labs for women. However, after

much (8)_____, Dr. Clapp convinced her college to

add more laboratories and more science classes. Later, she helped

establish the now-famous Marine Biology Lab at Woods Hole, on

Cape Cod. Dr. Clapp was truly a (9)_____ thinker.

Name _____

> **Helpful Hints**

The **suffix** en means "to make" or "become like."
   Pudding will **thick**en in the refrigerator.

The **suffix** ern gives a direction.
   The **south**ern part of Florida has storms.

The **suffix** ish means "belonging to a nation or people,"
"like," or "somewhat."
   Ir**ish** grandmother   boy**ish** face   redd**ish** brown

If a word ends in **silent** e, drop the e before adding **ish**.
   blue + ish = blu**ish**

Underline the suffix in each word below.

1. western   2. Swedish   3. babyish

4. whitish   5. straighten   6. northeastern

7. soften   8. Spanish   9. sharpen

Complete each sentence by using one of the words from the list above. Write a word only once.

10. If you are from Sweden, you are _____.

11. Use a ruler to _____ your lines.

12. Nail biting is a _____ habit.

13. In Spain, most people speak _____.

14. A movie about the Old West is called a _____.

15. New York and New Jersey are _____ states.

16. To make a pencil point sharper, you _____ it.

17. A paint that is somewhat white is _____.

18. You can _____ your clothes in the rinse cycle.

> **CHALLENGE**

The great doctor William Harvey discovered that the heart pumps blood through the body. What nationality was William Harvey? Unscramble the word below to find out. Then write a sentence using the word.

   sliehgn

Underline the suffix in each word in the box. Then write the correct word from the box to answer each question. Use a word only once.

eastern	English	straighten	southeastern	tallish
northwestern	golden	lengthen	darkish	darken	Turkish

1. Which word means "somewhat tall"? _____

2. Which direction is to the north and west? _____

3. Which word means "belonging to Turkey"? _____

4. Which direction means "toward the east? _____

5. Which word means "make darker"? _____

6. Which word means "somewhat dark"? _____

7. Which direction is to the south and east? _____

8. Which word means "belonging to England"? _____

9. Which word means "make straighter"? _____

10. Which word means "make longer"? _____

11. What do you call something with a gold color? _____

Complete each sentence. Use a word from the box above.

12. Alabama is in the _____ part of the United States.

13. Buildings that are somewhat tall are _____.

14. I love to eat _____ delight at fairs.

15. We need to _____ the circles on some of our tests.

16. The sun is a _____ color this morning.

LESSON 75: Suffixes **-en, -ern, -ish**

Home Involvement Activity Use a map to play *What Town Am I?* Take turns using direction words to describe the location of cities or towns on the map. Each person can ask two questions before guessing the place.

Name _____

Read each group of words below. Draw one line under the word that has a suffix. Then draw two lines under the suffix.

1. high humidity
2. will strengthen their case
3. yellowish in color
4. in an eastern county
5. won the election
6. Finnish cheese from Finland
7. a massive storm
8. waits for the clay to harden
9. a lightish color
10. wants more publicity
11. uses persuasion
12. would weaken their muscles
13. a Turkish towel
14. first city to use electricity

Underline the suffix in each of these words. Then write the number of syllables that the word has. Add the total number of syllables of all the words.

Thomas Edison with his "light bulb" invention in 1915

Syllables

15. invention _____
16. discussion _____
17. protective _____
18. widen _____
19. description _____
20. southwestern _____
21. British _____
22. plumpish _____
23. inferiority _____
24. babyish _____
25. education _____

Total: _____

WORK TOGETHER

Form a small group. One person keeps time for 2 minutes. Other group members list 2-syllable words and 3-syllable words, all with suffixes. Try to list a total of 10 words.

Underline the suffix in each word below. Then sort the words according to the number of syllables that the words have. Write each word in the correct column below.

reddish	fascination	reality
positive	impressive	publicity
education	toughen	disruptive
northern	attraction	tension
Polish	conclusion	observation

1 Has Two Syllables	2 Has Three Syllables	3 Has Four Syllables
_____	_____	_____
_____	_____	_____
_____	_____	_____
_____	_____	_____
_____	_____	_____

Answer each question. Write a word from the boxes above.

4. Which four-syllable word means "the act of observing"? _____

5. Which three-syllable word means "the act of attracting"? _____

6. Which two-syllable word means "belonging to Poland"? _____

7. Which four-syllable word means "the act of educating"? _____

8. Which two-syllable word means "to make tough"? _____

9. Which three-syllable word means "tending to impress"? _____

10. Which two-syllable word means "to the north"? _____

11. Which two-syllable word means "somewhat red"? _____

12. Which three-syllable word means "tending to disrupt"? _____

LESSON 76: Suffixes and Syllables

Home Involvement Activity Choose five words with suffixes. Write each word on an index card, with a scrambled version on the back. Challenge family members to unscramble the words.

⭐ **Read about a famous African American scientist and inventor.
Then answer the questions that follow.**

A Mind Like Clockwork

Benjamin Banneker (also spelled *Bannaker*) was born in Baltimore in 1731. Unlike most African Americans of his time, he was the son of free blacks. For a few winters, the young Banneker attended a small country school. That was all the formal education he ever had. Yet the boy had an active mind. He could understand the way things worked without being taught.

Banneker showed his genius for science by building a clock. He used only wooden parts that he invented himself. He built his clock without ever having seen a working clock. No one had told him how to do it. Banneker could teach himself whatever he wanted to learn. He was amazing.

When he was fifty-seven years old, Banneker taught himself advanced mathematics. He used this math and some instruments to learn how the planets, moon, stars, and comets move in space. He wrote a successful book about what he had learned.

Yet Banneker was more than a writer, an inventor, and a scientist. He was also an architect. In 1791, President George Washington began making plans for the nation's new capital—Washington, DC. George Washington hired Banneker to help plan the city.

By the time he died in 1806, Benjamin Banneker was famous. This great man was known for being a writer, an inventor, and a scientist. He was also famous for being the designer of a young nation's new capital.

📖 Reader's Response

1. **What was amazing about Benjamin Banneker?**

2. **Imagine that Banneker and Copernicus could meet. Do you think they would become friends? What would they have in common?**

3. **How are you like and unlike Benjamin Banneker? Do you like science? Do you teach yourself new things? Explain.**

Clocks are everywhere. There are old clocks, new clocks, big clocks, and hard-to-read clocks. There are clocks on the wall, on your wrist, and on the microwave oven. There are clocks that chime, that beep, and that sing. Think about the clocks that you see every day. How are they like and unlike one another? Which clock is your favorite? Why?

Describe your idea of the perfect clock. Tell what it looks like and what special things it can do. Use at least two of these words to write your description.

biggest   noisiest   measurement   quickly   easily   valuable   readable

soften   colorful   fascination   ability   attractive   electricity   clearly

_____

_____

_____

_____

_____

_____

_____

_____

_____

Writer's Tip

Bring your ideas to life. Use vivid words and details that will help your audience see, hear, and feel your description.

Writer's Challenge

Imagine that one day all the clocks stopped! Describe what the day would be like for you at school and at home. How would you get by without knowing the exact time? What might go wrong? Use different kinds of sentences to make your description more interesting.

Lesson 77: Connecting Reading and Writing
Comprehension—Compare and Contrast; Synthesize

Name _____

Helpful Hints

The **suffix** ward means "in a certain direction."

Eastward means "toward the east."
Downward means "in a lower direction."

The **suffix** less means "without."

Careless means "without care."

The **suffix** ship means "state or condition."

Friendship is the state of being friends.

Ship may also mean "office or rank of" or "ability or skill."

She won the **governor**ship by just a few votes.
Her **penman**ship is the best in the class.

French scientist
Louis Pasteur
(1822–1895) in
his laboratory

Read each group of words. Underline the suffix in each word in bold print.

1. pedal **backward**
2. a **harmless** prank
3. a strong **kinship**

4. a great **hardship**
5. an **upward** turn
6. a **tireless** worker

7. a **needless** expense
8. **westward** journey
9. a **hopeless** situation

Complete the sentences below. Choose from the words in bold print above.

10. The scientist Louis Pasteur led the _____ fight to discover what caused disease.

11. Years of research caused Pasteur great _____.

12. Yet one day, his research took an _____ turn.

13. Pasteur's research proved a strong _____ between germs and disease.

14. This great scientist proved that germs were not _____, but harmful.

CHALLENGE

The suffixes less and ful are opposites:

help**less**/help**ful**

pain**less**/pain**ful**

List two other base words to which you can add the suffixes less and ful.

⭐ **Underline the suffix you can add to each base word below. Then write the new word on the line.**

1. **name**   ward   less   _____

2. **citizen**   ship   less   _____

3. **age**   ship   less   _____

4. **out**   ship   ward   _____

5. **time**   ward   less   _____

6. **scholar**   ship   ward   _____

7. **down**   ship   ward   _____

8. **partner**   ship   ward   _____

9. **thought**   ship   less   _____

10. **in**   ward   less   _____

⭐ **Complete each sentence with a word from the box. Add the suffix ward, less, or ship to each word so that the sentence makes sense.**

citizen	count	friend	home	taste	sky

11. Look _____ at the hot-air balloons floating above.

12. There are _____ uses for aircraft.

13. The special _____ between the gorilla Koko and a kitten was told in an interesting book.

14. My horse seems to know when we ride in a _____ direction.

15. Babies born in the United States have American _____.

16. Adding garlic and salt may give the _____ soup some flavor.

Home Involvement Activity Invite family members to discuss the true meaning of **friend**ship. Encourage them to use some of the words from this lesson, such as **kin**ship, **time**less, and **partner**ship.

Name _____

> **Helpful Hints**

The **suffixes** er, or, and ist mean "someone who makes or does something."

   A **teacher** is someone who teaches.

   An **inventor** is someone who invents.

   A **cartoonist** is someone who draws cartoons.

If the **base word** ends in **silent** e, drop the e before adding er, or, or ist.

   dance → dancer   create → creator   type → typist

If a **base word** has a short vowel sound, double the final consonant before adding a suffix.

   ship → shipper   log → logger

Underline the suffix in each of these careers. Then write the meaning of the word on the blank line.

1. artist   _____

2. producer   _____

3. director   _____

4. reporter   _____

Write a word from the box to complete each sentence.

| chemist | inventor | journalist | painter |

5. Pablo Picasso was a modern _____.

6. A _____ in Germany made the first aspirin powder.

7. Josephine Cochrane was the _____ of the dishwasher.

8. The author of *The Wizard of Oz* began his career

   as a newspaper _____.

> **CHALLENGE**

Scientists are people who practice or study science.

What areas of science do these people study? Use a dictionary to help you.

   geologist
   volcanologist
   zoologist

Solve each clue. Write one letter in each space. Then read down the shaded column to write the answer to the question below.

1. What singers do   _ _ _ _

2. Dial "0" to reach this person   _ _ _ _ _ _ _ _

3. What creators do   _ _ _ _ _ _

4. Where scuba divers explore   _ _ _ _ _

5. The instrument a pianist plays   _ _ _ _ _

6. Where a gardener works   _ _ _ _ _ _

7. What a violinist plays   _ _ _ _ _ _ _

8. Someone who makes art   _ _ _ _ _ _

9. What swimmers do   _ _ _ _

10. What a batter hits with   _ _ _

Question: What do you call people who focus on one subject or area and become experts in it?

Answer: This person is called a _____.

Think about people you admire. Write your answers on the lines.

11. Name your favorite singer.

_____

12. Name your favorite actor.

_____

13. Name your favorite player (in any sport).

_____

14. Name your favorite writer.

_____

15. Name your favorite inventor.

_____

In 1903, the Wright Brothers made the first successful flight in this motor-powered airplane, which they invented.

Home Involvement Activity Some English last names, such as **Baker, Cooper, Miller,** or **Singer,** came from the work people did. List other job-related names. Do you know people who have the names you have listed?

Name _____

> **Helpful Hints**

The **suffixes** ance, dom, and ism mean "the act, state, quality, condition, or result of." The **suffix** dom may also mean "office, rank, or realm," as in **king**dom.

Assistance is the act of assisting or helping.
Freedom is the state of being free.
Heroism is the actions or qualities of a hero.

Guion S. Bluford, an example of **heroism**

Underline the suffix in each word below.

1. boredom
2. inheritance
3. attendance

4. disturbance
5. patriotism
6. kingdom

7. resemblance
8. wisdom
9. importance

10. criticism
11. guidance
12. terrorism

Read each phrase. Then unscramble the letters in bold print to form one of the words from the list above. Write the unscrambled word on the line.

13. the **dwomsi** of the elderly chief _____

14. peace throughout the **modnigk** _____

15. received **digceanu** from her family _____

16. stressed the **ipmoatrcen** of honesty _____

17. yawning from **droombe** _____

18. daily **tacentaedn** taken in class _____

19. the **mistoirtap** of George Washington _____

20. a loud **transdicube** _____

21. a striking **ancesembler** _____

> **CHALLENGE**

The noun **elegance** is related to the adjective **elegant**. What adjective is each of these nouns related to?

brilliance
fragrance
importance

Underline the suffix in each word in bold print. Then draw a line to match the word with its definition. Write the letter of the definition on the blank line.

_____ 1. **magnetism**   a. the act of assisting or helping

_____ 2. **freedom**   b. the act of criticizing or making judgments

_____ 3. **annoyance**   c. the act of annoying; being annoyed

_____ 4. **hypnotism**   d. the act of destroying property

_____ 5. **assistance**   e. the act of putting someone into a sleeplike state

_____ 6. **criticism**   f. the state of being insured

_____ 7. **heroism**   g. the actions or qualities of a hero

_____ 8. **vandalism**   h. the quality of being wise

_____ 9. **wisdom**   i. the state of being free

_____ 10. **insurance**   j. the quality of being magnetic, or attracting

Use each of the words in bold print above. Write a sentence that shows the meaning of each word.

11. _____

12. _____

13. _____

14. _____

15. _____

16. _____

17. _____

18. _____

19. _____

20. _____

LESSON 80: Suffixes **-ance, -dom, -ism**

Home Involvement Activity Discuss the meaning of the word **free**dom. Talk about the kinds of freedoms that are important to your family—and to the nation.

Name _____

⭐ **Add** the suffix ern to two of the following base words. Add the suffix ance to the other two. Then write a sentence for each word.

Base Word	Word with Suffix	Sentence
1. guide	_____	_____
2. west	_____	_____
3. disturb	_____	_____
4. northeast	_____	_____

⭐ **Add** the suffix less to two of the following base words. Add the suffix dom to the other two. Then write a sentence for each word.

Base Word	Word with Suffix	Sentence
5. free	_____	_____
6. harm	_____	_____
7. pain	_____	_____
8. wise	_____	_____

⭐ **Add** the suffix ish to one of the following base words. Add the suffix ist to the other one. Then write a sentence for each word.

Base Word	Word with Suffix	Sentence
9. tall	_____	_____
10. journal	_____	_____

⭐ **Add** the suffix ism to one of the following base words. Add the suffix or to the other one. Then write a sentence for each word.

Base Word	Word with Suffix	Sentence
11. invent	_____	_____
12. hero	_____	_____

Read the sentences. Choose a word from the box that completes each sentence correctly. Then write the word on the line.

kingdom	Swedish	scientists	importance

1. How do _____ sort living things into groups that make sense?

2. Long ago, a _____ man named Linnaeus came up with a plan.

3. He saw the _____ of finding out how living things are alike.

4. He sorted all life forms into the animal or the plant _____.

Choose a word from the box that has a different suffix from the word in bold print. Write a sentence that uses both words. An example is given below.

actor _____ The **actor** played the part of the **scientist**.

conductor	heroism	teacher	scientist	guidance

5. **dancer** _____

_____

6. **sailor** _____

_____

7. **leadership** _____

_____

8. **wisdom** _____

_____

Extend & Apply

Place the four terms below in an order that makes sense.
All the terms belong to the animal kingdom. List them from
the most general to the most exact, or specific.

Welsh terrier   mammal   dog   terrier

Name _____

Helpful Hints

The **suffix** some means "like" or "tending to be."
A **tire**some buzz can make you sleepy.

The **suffix** hood means "state, quality, or condition of."
Dad spent his **boy**hood in Japan.

The **suffix** most means "greatest or closest to."
DNA is found in the **inner**most part of our cells.

Computer model of DNA

Join each base word and suffix. Write the new word on the line.

1. outer + most   _____

2. false + hood   _____

3. trouble + some   _____

4. child + hood   _____

5. lone + some   _____

6. top + most   _____

7. fear + some   _____

8. neighbor + hood _____

Complete each sentence. Use a word from the list above.

9. The _____ layer is the farthest out.

10. Six students in our class live on the same street in the

    same _____.

11. A _____ problem fills you with worry.

12. A lion can be a _____ sight.

13. Being _____ is not the same thing
    as being alone.

CHALLENGE

The word **utmost** ends with the suffix most. Find out the meaning of **utmost**. Then describe in a sentence your utmost wish or hope.

⭐ **Complete each statement. Write your answer on the line.**

1. Name a sport that can be played by a twosome. _____

2. Name a game that a threesome can play. _____

3. What game can be played by a foursome? _____

4. What sport can a foursome play? _____

⭐ **Think about good answers to the following questions. Write your answers on the lines. If you are unsure of the meaning of a word in bold print, check a dictionary.**

5. How might you deal with a **quarrelsome** person?

   _____

   _____

6. What will you find at the **westernmost** border of your state?

   _____

   _____

7. Which is your favorite street in your **neighborhood**? Tell why.

   _____

   _____

8. Tell about a time when you felt **lonesome**.

   _____

   _____

LESSON 82: Suffixes **-some**,
-hood, -most

 Home Involvement Activity Have a family discussion.
Talk about the challenges and joys of **parent**hood and
the challenges and joys of **child**hood. Compare and
contrast these stages of life.

Name _____

> **Helpful Hint**
>
> Some words have more than one **suffix**.
> The word **fear**lessly has the suffixes less + ly.
> The word **help**fulness has the suffixes ful + ness.

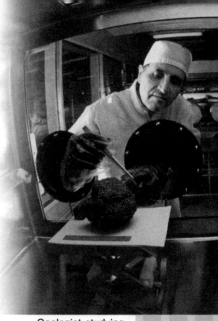

Geologist studying
a lunar rock

★ **Each of these words has two suffixes. Draw one line under the first suffix and two lines under the second suffix.**

1. skillfully   2. enjoyably   3. carelessness

4. loneliness   5. thoughtfulness   6. defensively

7. juiciness   8. wholesomeness   9. governorship

★ **Underline the word that has more than one suffix in each sentence. Then draw two lines under each suffix. Write the base word on the line below.**

10. Their inventions were filled with creativity.

    _____

11. We spoke respectfully about their work.

    _____

12. Their childishness was annoying sometimes.

    _____

13. Don't behave foolishly while working.

    _____

14. Scientists need to work carefully.

    _____

15. Act thoughtlessly and you might get hurt.

    _____

16. That lab is in the northernmost part of the state.

    _____

> **CHALLENGE**
>
> Write a word with more than one suffix to complete this sentence.
>
> His _____ *made him a good worker.*
>
> How many different words can you think of? Make a list.

Some words have both a **prefix** and a **suffix**.
The word **dis**agree**ment** is made up of the prefix **dis**,
the suffix **ment**, and the base word **agree**.

Write the prefix, the base word, and the suffix for each word below.
Use + signs to separate the three parts. You may need to change the
spelling of some base words. The first one is done for you.

1. bicyclist _____ bi + cycle + ist _____

2. refillable _____

3. overactivity _____

4. nonviolently _____

5. disgraceful _____

6. coworker _____

7. unfriendly _____

8. mismanagement _____

9. enjoyable _____

Family on Four Position Bicycle

Fill in the circle of the word that completes each sentence
correctly. Then write the word on the line.

10. Luckily, the new clothes we bought were _____.
    ○ disgraceful   ○ exchangeable   ○ unfriendly

11. The company hired a _____ for the sick worker.
    ○ replacement   ○ refillable   ○ returnable

12. Their _____ was over what to wear to the dance.
    ○ refreshment   ○ disagreement   ○ nonpayment

13. Our _____ guaranteed that no one else could
    buy the car.
    ○ prepayment   ○ refundable   ○ thoughtlessness

14. The principal disapproved of the children's _____ behavior.
    ○ enjoyable   ○ immaturity   ○ disagreeable

Home Involvement Activity Look through newspapers
or magazines. Find as many words as you can that have
two or more suffixes or a prefix and a suffix. Post the
words that you find on a Word Wall.

Name _____

- When a word ends in **silent** e, usually drop the e before adding a **suffix** that starts with a vowel.

  nice→nic**est**   typ**e**→typ**ist**   inflate→inflat**able**

- When a word ends in le, drop the le before adding the **suffix** ly.

  reliab**le**→reliab**ly**   humb**le**→humb**ly**   possib**le**→possib**ly**

- When a word ends in y after a consonant, change the y to i before adding a **suffix**. But *do not* change the y to i if the suffix begins with i.

  hap**py**→happ**iness**   thir**ty**→thirt**yish**   beau**ty**→beaut**iful**

Scientist Marie Curie (1867–1934) working in her laboratory in 1905

Use the base word and the suffix to write a new word.

1. cute + est _____

2. dive + er _____

3. foggy + er _____

4. baby + ish _____

5. store + age _____

6. erase + able _____

7. plenty + ful _____

8. bubble + ly _____

9. steady + est _____

10. adore + able _____

CHALLENGE

Some words may not always follow the spelling rules.

How would you spell these words? Look in a dictionary to check your answers.

love + able
exchange + able
knowledge + able

Draw a line to connect each base word with a suffix to form three words. Then write the words on the lines. Spell the words correctly.

11		12		13	
cure	y	bounty	able	prank	en
create	able	happy	ful	loose	ful
rose	ive	rely	est	care	ish

_____   _____   _____

_____   _____   _____

_____   _____   _____

- When a one-syllable word with a short vowel sound ends in a single consonant, double that consonant before you add a **suffix** that begins with a vowel.

    hot→hottest   swim→swimmer   sad→sadden

But if that one-syllable word ends in x, *do not* double the x.

    box→boxer   tax→taxable

- When a two-syllable word is accented on the second syllable, treat it as you would a one-syllable word. Usually double the consonant before you add a suffix that begins with a vowel.

    forget→forgettable   admit→admittance

Use the base word and the suffix to write a new word on the line. Be sure to follow the spelling rules.

1. mad + er _____
2. Scot + ish _____
3. remit + ance _____
4. slim + est _____
5. flop + y _____
6. mix + er _____
7. wet + est _____
8. run + er _____
9. fix + er _____
10. box + y _____
11. fat + en _____
12. hit + er _____

Circle the suffix in each word in bold print. Then write the base word on the line.

13. Before 1955, polio was one of the medical world's

    biggest problems. _____

14. Dr. Jonas Salk discovered an **acceptable** way to

    fight polio. _____

15. The Salk vaccine protected people from getting

    this **regrettable** disease. _____

Dr. Jonas Salk (1914–1995)
in his laboratory

 Home Involvement Activity Work together to write a brief paragraph about the importance of caring for your health. Use as many suffixes as you can. Check your spelling in a dictionary or a spell-checker.

Name _____

⭐ **Read what *Apollo* astronaut Alan L. Bean has to say about his career and about future careers in space. Then answer the questions that follow.**

Your Future in Space

by Alan L. Bean

When John Glenn became the first American to orbit Earth on Feb. 20, 1962, I was a pilot at the Naval Air Test Center in Patuxent River, MD. I tested planes like the *F-4A Phantom Two* and *A-3J Vigilante* that flew twice the speed of sound. I thought I had the hottest job in the Navy—indeed, the world.

I listened on the radio as the *Atlas* rocket successfully boosted Glenn's *Mercury* capsule into space. Then I climbed into a *Skyhawk* for a short test hop. By the time I landed, Glenn was preparing to splash down in the Pacific after circling the planet three times. Quickly, I calculated that during the time it took me to fly 1,000 miles, Glenn went 36,000! I began to realize that somebody else might have a more interesting job.

Later that year, when the National Aeronautics and Space Administration announced plans to hire more astronauts, I applied but was not selected. I applied again one year later, and NASA accepted me. In 1969, I became the fourth man to walk on the Moon.

When I ventured into space, the only route was by learning to fly. As we explore space in the future, we will need pilots, technicians, scientists and probably people with jobs nobody has yet described. When you think about space, it's hard to dream too big a dream.

📖 Reader's Response

1. **Why did Alan L. Bean decide to become an astronaut?**

2. **What would you say in a summary of this article?**

3. **Do you think you might decide to become an astronaut or another kind of space scientist someday? Give three reasons for your answer.**

Astronaut Alan L. Bean says that when he was growing up, his great love was airplanes. He never dreamed that one day he would have a career in space. Bean also realizes that as we continue to explore space, we will need more scientists. We will also probably need "people with jobs nobody has yet described."

Imagine that you have applied for a job that "nobody has yet described." Write a paragraph that tells about this new job. Describe what you would do and where and how you would do it. Use at least two of these words in your job description.

usable   useless   inventor   scientist   easily   effortless   protective

helpful   equipment   straighten   ability   attractive   valuable   clearly

_____

_____

_____

_____

_____

_____

_____

_____

_____

Writer's Tip

Add some simple drawings or diagrams to help your readers understand your job.

Beyond a Young Boy's Dream, painting by Alan L. Bean

Speaker's Challenge

Write and tell a riddle that describes a real job, but don't name the job in your riddle. Challenge a partner to guess what your mystery job is. Vary your tone of voice to stress important clues.

Name _____

⭐ **Look at the word-part chart below. Use it to form words. You can form the word happiness by combining C2 + G3.**

	1	2	3
A	im	help	ful
B	mid	create	ment
C	over	happy	ish
D	mis	joy	able
E	co	life	less
F	pre	name	like
G	dis	possible	ness
H	en	measure	ion
I	re	grace	ly
J	un	accept	est
K	in	friend	ive

A **volcanologist** taking measurements of the Mayon volcano in the Philippines

⭐ **Use the word-part chart to decode these words. Then write the words on the lines. Make spelling changes as needed.**

1. H2 + B3 _____

2. E2 + F3 _____

3. I2 + A3 _____

4. I1 + F2 _____

5. A2 + E3 _____

6. B2 + K3 _____

7. C2 + J3 _____

8. F2 + E3 _____

9. J1 + K2 + I3 _____

10. J1 + J2 + D3 _____

11. A1 + G2 + I3 _____

12. H1 + D2 + B3 _____

⭐ **Use the word-part chart to encode these words. Write the letters and the numbers on the lines.**

13. joyful _____

14. enjoyable _____

15. lifeless _____

16. disgraceful _____

17. overcreative _____

18. mismeasurement _____

Read the passage. For each numbered blank, there is a choice of words below. Circle the letter of the word that completes the sentence correctly.

Maria's class was studying volcanoes. The students wanted to build a model of one. They wanted their volcano to look **1**. Therefore, the class asked the art teacher for **2**.

First, she told them to make a dome-shaped frame out of wire. She helped them mount it on the **3** base they had. Then the students tore long strips of newspaper and soaked them in wheat paste. They put layers of paper onto the wire frame to make it look like a mountain.

When the model was dry, the students painted it. They hid a jar inside the mountaintop to hold **4** materials for the eruption. The jar held soap, paint, glitter, and baking soda. Then the students poured in some vinegar and—boom! The volcano came to life! It squirted a reddish liquid. The <u>lava</u> ran **5** toward the base.

1. **a.** lifelike   **b.** lifeless   **c.** graceful

2. **a.** kindness   **b.** assistance   **c.** baggage

3. **a.** happiest   **b.** sturdiest   **c.** tiresome

4. **a.** childish   **b.** falsehood   **c.** colorful

5. **a.** downward   **b.** upward   **c.** northern

Read the passage again. Circle the letter of your answer.

6. **Why did the students ask the art teacher for help?**
   a. She liked studying about science.
   b. She knew model-building methods.
   c. She had been to the Philippines.
   d. She was a nature photographer.

7. **What does the word <u>lava</u> mean?**
   a. toothpaste
   b. watery dirt
   c. rare chemicals
   d. hot, red liquid rock

Extend & Apply

Gather information about a volcano to share with your classmates. Write a fact sheet that has at least one word with a suffix.

Happy Birthday, U.S.A.!

Did you know that countries have birthdays? Every year on July 4, Americans celebrate Independence Day. On this day, we hold big parades and watch colorful fireworks displays. We sing patriotic songs and fly the American flag. Do you know what happened on July 4 to make this day our national birthday?

A daring event took place in Philadelphia on July 4, 1776. On that hot summer day, the members of the Continental Congress took a bold step. They signed a paper that called for independence from England. These 56 people signed the Declaration of Independence with pride—and some fear. John Hancock was the first to sign. He wrote his name in bold letters. Benjamin Franklin also signed. Thomas Jefferson, the author of the Declaration of Independence, signed, too.

Today, we still value this great document. We can see it on display in the National Archives building in Washington, DC. It is the place where the government keeps records of our nation's history. Just visit the National Archives building on the Fourth of July. It is open on that day for all to say, "Happy Birthday, U.S.A.!"

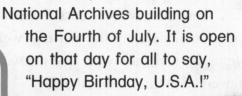

? Critical Thinking

1. **What do we celebrate on Independence Day?**

2. **What could have made the signers of the Declaration of Independence feel both pride and fear?**

3. **Do you think it is important for a nation to keep records of its past? Why?**

LESSON 87: Introduction to Dictionary and Thesaurus Skills; Synonyms, Antonyms, Homonyms; Clipped, Blended, and Borrowed Words; Idioms and Analogies

177

Word Study at Home

**Visit us at
www.sadlier-oxford.com**

Dear Family,

Your child has begun Unit 6 of Sadlier's *Word Study* program. Lessons in this unit focus on dictionary and thesaurus skills; on synonyms, antonyms, and homonyms; on clipped, blended, and borrowed words; and on idioms and analogies. The theme of this unit is *people and government*.

Synonyms are words that have the same or nearly the same meaning (**freezing** and **cold**).

Antonyms are words that have opposite meanings (**hot** and **cold**).

Homonyms are words that sound the same but have different meanings and different spellings (**ate/eight**).

Clipped words are shorter forms of words (hamburger→burger).

Blended words combine two words by leaving out letters (**sm**oke + f**og** = smog).

Happy Birthday, U.S.A.!

Did you know that countries have birthdays? Every year on July 4, Americans celebrate Independence Day. On this day, we hold big parades and watch colorful fireworks displays. We sing patriotic songs and fly the American flag. Do you know what happened on July 4 to make this day our national birthday?

A daring event took place in Philadelphia on July 4, 1776. On that hot summer day, the members of the Continental Congress took a bold step. They signed a paper that called for independence from England. These 56 people signed the Declaration of Independence with pride—and some fear. John Hancock was the first to sign. He wrote his name in bold letters. Benjamin Franklin also signed. Thomas Jefferson, the author of the Declaration of Independence, signed, too.

Today, we still value this great document. We can see it on display in the National Archives building in Washington, DC. It is the place where the government keeps records of our nation's history. Just visit the National Archives building on the Fourth of July. It is open on that day for all to say, "Happy Birthday, U.S.A.!"

Critical Thinking

1. What do we celebrate on Independence Day?
2. What could have made the signers of the Declaration of Independence feel both pride and fear?
3. Do you think it is important for a nation to keep records of its past? Why?

LESSON 87: Introduction to Dictionary and Thesaurus Skills; Synonyms, Antonyms, Homonyms; Clipped, Blended, and Borrowed Words; Idioms and Analogies   177

Family Focus

- Post a "Word of the Day" in your home. Choose a funny word, an odd word, or a word from the news. Discuss the meaning and pronunciation of the word, as well as any synonyms and antonyms. Use the word in conversation throughout the day.

- Read the passage on page 177 and talk about it together. How does your family celebrate Independence Day? What memories of this holiday can you share?

LINKS TO LEARNING

Web Sites
www.nara.gov

www.july4thparade.com

Videos
Inside the White House, National Geographic Video.

Our National Parks, PBS Home Video.

Literature
The Hatmaker's Sign, a story by Benjamin Franklin, retold by Candace Fleming, ©1998.

Our Declaration of Independence by Jay Schleifer, ©1992.

Rights and Responsibilities by Lila Summer and Samuel D. Woods, ©1977.

Name _____

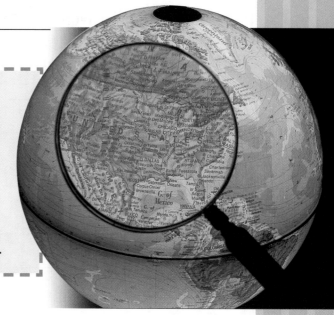

Helpful Hint

Words in a dictionary are arranged in **ABC order**, or **alphabetical order**. To put words in ABC order, look at the first letter of each word. If the first letter is the same, look at the next letter to decide the order.

The names of these cities are in ABC order.

Dayton   Denver   Detroit   Dover

Write each group of words in ABC order.

1. state _____

   country _____

   governor _____

   region _____

2. congress _____

   bill _____

   vote _____

   veto _____

Figure out this riddle. Write the next letter of the alphabet above each letter in the box. Then write the riddle's question and answer on the lines below.

								A											A		A					
V	G	D	Q	D		V	R		S	G	D		C	D	B	K		Q		S	H	N	M

																							?
N	E		H	M	C	D	O	D	M	C	D	M	B	D		R	H	F	M	D	C		

A	T											!
			S	G	D		A	N	S	S	N	L

Question: _____

Answer: _____

CHALLENGE

Create a sentence that uses **ABC order**, such as: Abe buys cat food. Make your sentence as long as you can.

⭐ **Write each group of words in ABC order.**

1. Capitol   _____

   captain   _____

   city   _____

   capital   _____

2. borough   _____

   build   _____

   borrow   _____

   butter   _____

3. senator   _____

   sentence   _____

   senate   _____

   supervisor   _____

4. president   _____

   present   _____

   pleasant   _____

   presence   _____

⭐ **These states begin with the letter M or N. Use the chart below to sort the states by letter. Then put the states in ABC order by numbering them from *1–8*. Write the numbers on the short lines in each column.**

Maryland	Montana	North Carolina	Missouri
New York	New Mexico	Nevada	Massachusetts
Michigan	North Dakota	New Jersey	Nebraska
Maine	Minnesota	Mississippi	New Hampshire

5 M	6 N
____ _____	____ _____
____ _____	____ _____
____ _____	____ _____
____ _____	____ _____
____ _____	____ _____
____ _____	____ _____
____ _____	____ _____
____ _____	____ _____

LESSON 88: ABC Order

Home Involvement Activity Eight states begin with the letter M. Eight other states begin with the letter N. Four states begin with the letter A, I, or W. Which states are they? Look at a map to see if you're right.

Name ______________________________

Helpful Hint

Two **guide words** appear at the top of each dictionary page. They show the first and last entries on that page. The other words on the dictionary page appear in alphabetical order between those two guide words.

Read the guide words in bold print. Cross out the one word that would *not* be on the same dictionary page as the guide words. Then write the three words in ABC order.

1 **oat / ore**	2 **sense / spoon**	3 **diplomat / director**
oar	sour	direct
opera	sister	direction
omen	sport	dipper
oh	sloppy	diploma
______	______	______
______	______	______
______	______	______

4 **mass / mice**	5 **bread / bridle**
measure	breed
mature	breath
marvelous	break
meow	brim
______	______
______	______
______	______

WORK TOGETHER

Choose a partner. Ask each other riddles, such as: "I am a word found on a page with the guide words **hectic—helpless.**" I mean "assistant." What am I? Check your answer in a dictionary.

⭐ **Write each word from the box under the correct guide words.**

peach	presto	plum	party	plot	pearl
presume	pencil	poem	prestige	pest	
plenty	pressure	poach	pretend	peasant	
platter	press	phonics	please	preteen	

1 pantry / picture

_____
_____
_____
_____
_____
_____
_____

2 plate / post

_____
_____
_____
_____
_____
_____
_____

3 president / pretty

_____
_____
_____
_____
_____
_____
_____

⭐ **Read each sentence. Underline the word that would appear in a dictionary between the guide words at the left.**

sense / sincere

4. Some American Presidents serve two four-year terms.

narrow / nationwide

5. The First Lady naturally focuses on national issues.

almost / alter

6. Presidents also have full-time assistants.

imp / impress

7. The Press Secretary is an important member of the President's staff.

chance / civil

8. Presidents choose people to be members of the Cabinet.

gesture / giddy

9. Presidents hope to get good advice.

chin / clout

10. The President may also choose Supreme Court judges.

 Home Involvement Activity How many pages does your dictionary have? How many guide words? About how many entry words are there on a page? Do the math together.

Name _____

> ## Helpful Hint
>
> Think of the dictionary as having three parts.
>
> The words in the **beginning** part start with the letters A–I.
> The words in the **middle** start with the letters J–Q.
> The words in the **end** part start with the letters R–Z.
>
> Turn to the beginning, the middle, or the end of the dictionary to help you quickly find words.

⭐ **Sort the words according to the part of the dictionary in which you would find each word.**

debate	treasury	lawyer	court
judge	voter	district	jury	tax

1 **Beginning:** A–I	2 **Middle:** J–Q	3 **End:** R–Z
_____	_____	_____
_____	_____	_____
_____	_____	_____

⭐ **Each sentence below has a word in bold print. Write *beginning*, *middle*, or *end* to tell in which part of the dictionary you would find the word.**

4. The nation had economic **troubles** after the

   American Revolution. _____

5. The **country** had borrowed money to fight.

   _____

6. To raise **money**, the new government increased

   the property tax. _____

> ## CHALLENGE
>
> Write the words from each sentence that would appear in the same part of the dictionary as the word in bold print.

Write *Beginning*, *Middle*, or *End* to tell in which part of the dictionary you would find each numbered word. Write A–I for the beginning letters, J–Q for the middle letters, and R–Z for the end letters. Then circle the correct pair of *guide words* below that would appear on the same page as the numbered word.

1. **sheriff** _____
   shift/shop   shame/shield   sift/silly

2. **census** _____
   central/ceramic   celebrate/cell   cement/center

3. **volunteer** _____
   violet/vote   valiant/value   valve/vanilla

4. **nation** _____
   narrator/nasty   nasal/navy   natural/neighbor

5. **general** _____
   garlic/gem   geology/ginger   geese/giant

6. **kingdom** _____
   kimono/knife   kettle/kilogram   knob/knuckle

7. **supervisor** _____
   support/sweatshirt sound/sudden   suitcase/supper

8. **brass** _____
   brave/bridge   bowl/branch   brace/broadcast

9. **office** _____
   odor/official   odd/offhand   often/old

10. **worker** _____
   wood/work   workout/worldwide   work/workshop

Read the words in the box. Imagine that they are on the same page of a dictionary and that two of the words are guide words. Which would be the first guide word? Which would be the second?

```
conquer    coyote    connect    compete    congress

connection    content    craft    court    courtroom
```

11. First guide word: _____   12. Second guide word: _____

Name _____

Helpful Hints

Words given in a dictionary are called **entry words**. Entry words appear in bold print in **ABC order.** The information about an entry word (its syllables, pronunciation, part of speech, definition, and other information) is called the **entry**.

Many words that have **endings**, **prefixes**, or **suffixes** will not appear as separate entry words. You may need to figure out the **base word** to know which entry word to look up.

splitting→**split**   rapidly→**rapid**   freshness→**fresh**

The Library of Congress

Read each word. Write the entry word you would look up in the dictionary to find the word. Use a dictionary to help you.

1. connected _____
2. discoveries _____
3. nearest _____
4. flavorful _____
5. nonsense _____
6. brainy _____
7. replaster _____
8. terribly _____

Helpful Hint

Some dictionaries have entry words for **abbreviations** and **contractions**. These entry words are listed in alphabetical order as if they were entire words.

Use a dictionary to write the word or words that each abbreviation and contraction stands for.

9. ave. _____
lb. _____
in. _____

10. I've _____ _____
it's _____ _____
doesn't _____ _____

CHALLENGE

Use a dictionary. Write two meanings for each of these abbreviations:

Mt.
DC
Dr.
Sr.

Sample Dictionary Entries

chasm A deep crack or opening in the earth's surface.
chasm (kaz'əm) *noun, plural* **chasms.**

jubilant Feeling or showing great joy. The players were *jubilant* over their victory.
ju•bi•lant (jü'bə lənt) *adjective.*

malaria A disease that causes chills, a high fever, and sweating. Malaria is spread by the bite of a certain type of mosquito that carries the disease from infected persons.
ma•lar•i•a (mə lâr' ē ə) *noun.*

pony express A postal service in which relays of riders on horseback carried mail across the western United States. The pony express ran from 1860 to 1861.

sieve A utensil that has a bottom with many holes in it. A sieve is used for sifting or draining.
sieve (siv) *noun, plural* **sieves.**

⭐ **Read the five dictionary entries above. Then write the entry word that fits each clue.**

1. This tool is used for sifting or draining. _____

2. You should take care never to fall into one of these. _____

3. You might feel this way if you won a tough contest. _____

4. Some kinds of mosquitoes can spread this sickness. _____

5. You could have worked for this postal service in 1860. _____

⭐ **Write your own sentence for each of the five entry words above.**

6. _____

7. _____

8. _____

9. _____

10. _____

 Home Involvement Activity Suppose that the name of each member of your family appeared in a dictionary. What entry word would appear just before the name? Just after? Look in a dictionary to find out.

Name _____

Helpful Hint

Some entry words have more than one meaning. Each different meaning is numbered. A word with more than one meaning is called a **homograph**. Homographs are **multiple-meaning words**.

Read each dictionary entry. Then read the sentences below it. On the line, write the number of the definition that fits the meaning of the word in bold print in the sentence.

elect 1. To choose by voting. The people *elected* a new governor.
2. To choose or decide. Will you *elect* to study Spanish in school?

1. Each November, our citizens have the chance to **elect** new leaders. _____

2. Would you **elect** to spend the summer at a computer camp or a

   baseball camp? _____

soak 1. To make very wet. We were *soaked* by the sudden rainstorm.
2. To absorb. The paper towel *soaked* up the spilled milk.
3. To let something stay in water. She left the dishes to *soak*.

3. If you **soak** your sweater, the stain may come out. _____

4. Our clothes were completely **soaked** by

   the thunderstorm. _____

5. Young children seem to **soak** up everything that

   people around them do. _____

teller 1. A person who tells or relates. Our librarian is a wonderful *teller* of tales. 2. A person who works in a bank and takes or gives out money.

6. Six **tellers** work at the First National Bank. _____

7. Grandpa is a talented **teller** of funny stories. _____

WORD STRATEGY

Multiple-meaning words may act as different parts of speech. What do these two words mean as a noun? As a verb?

   coat
   hail

Helpful Hint

Homographs are **multiple-meaning words** that have more than one dictionary entry. Homographs are spelled the same but have different meanings. You can identify homographs by the small raised number after them.

league¹ A number of people, groups, or nations joined together for a common purpose or goal.

league² A measure of distance that is equal to about three miles.

⭐ **Read the meanings of the homographs below. Then decide which word to use to complete each sentence. Write the word and its number on the line.**

alight¹ To come down from the air and settle on land.

alight² Lit up; glowing.

bear¹ To hold up; support the weight of.

bear² A large, heavy animal having long, shaggy hair.

case¹ An instance of something.

case² A box for holding something.

fast¹ Rapidly; quickly.

fast² To eat little or no food.

1. Members of the press wait to ask the President questions the moment he _____ from his special helicopter.

2. The sky is _____ with fireworks to welcome the President.

3. In most _____, the press wants to get details about the trip.

4. The President may have to give _____ answers in order to be on time for his next appointment.

5. The President of the United States must _____ many responsibilities.

6. Many of the President's papers are on display in a glass _____.

7. President Theodore Roosevelt liked to tell stories about grizzly _____.

8. Bears sleep during the winter, and they will _____ for several months.

🏠 **Home Involvement Activity** For each of these homographs, work together to write one sentence that uses two meanings of the word: **firm, kind, tire, jam, page,** and **saw.**

Name _____

Helpful Hints

Dictionaries have a **pronunciation key** at the beginning of the book and usually at the bottom of every other right-hand page. The pronunciation key uses letters, symbols, and sample words to help you pronounce the entry words.

Each dictionary entry gives a **respelling** of the entry word, usually inside parentheses ( ). The respelling uses the pronunciation key to show you how to say the word.

joy (joi)   judgment (juj′ mənt)   pony (pō′ nē)

Pronunciation Key–Bottom of Dictionary Page

at; āpe; fär; câre; end; mē; it; īce; pîerce; hot; ōld; sông, fôrk; oil; out; up; ūse; rüle; pull; tûrn; chin; sing; shop; thin; this; hw in white; zh in treasure. The symbol ə stands for the unstressed vowel sound in about, taken, pencil, lemon, and circus.

Read each sentence. Use the pronunciation key to help you say each respelled word in parentheses ( ). Then write the correct spelling for each of the words. Refer to the words in the box if you are not sure of the correct spelling.

> charge   judge   views   people   named   law

1. A (**juj**) makes decisions in court. _____

2. Some judges are elected by the (**pē′ pəl**). _____

3. Supreme Court Judges are (**nāmd**) by the President.

   _____

4. A judge must be an expert in the (**lô**). _____

5. The judge is in (**chärj**) of the courtroom. _____

6. Judges must put aside their personal (**vūz**) to

   rule fairly. _____

CHALLENGE

Four Presidents' names are respelled here. Write them as they are usually spelled.

ling′ kən

hāz

tī′ lər

pōk

The **pronunciation key** in a dictionary shows the sound of each vowel and some consonants. Look at this part of a pronunciation key from the front of a dictionary. It gives the sound of each vowel as well as sample words that have that vowel sound.

Read each respelling below. Next to it, write the word from the pronunciation key that has the same vowel sound. Then write the correct spelling for the word. The first one is done for you.

Respelling	Example Words with Same Vowel Sound	Correct Spelling
1 (boi)	oil, toy	boy
2 (brāv)		
3 (fôrs)		
4 (chärm)		
5 (drô)		
6 (skâr)		
7 (bùk)		
8 (wind)		
9 (yîr)		
10 (prün)		
11 (blēch)		
12 (bout)		
13 (rist)		

Pronunciation Key– Front of Dictionary

a — at, bad
ā — ape, pain, day, break
ä — father, car, heart
âr — care, pair, bear, their, where
e — end, pet, said, heaven, friend
ē — equal, me, feet, team, piece, key
i — it, big, English, hymn
ī — ice, fine, lie, my
îr — ear, deer, here, pierce
o — odd, hot, watch
ō — old, oat, toe, low
ô — coffee, all, taught, law, fought
ôr — order, fork, horse, story, pour
oi — oil, toy
ou — out, now
u — up, mud, love, double
ū — use, mule, cue, feud, few
ü — rule, true, food
ù — put, wood, should
ûr — burn, hurry, term, bird, word, courage
ə — about, taken, pencil, lemon, circus

Home Involvement Activity You will hear the **schwa sound** (ə) in many words. Work together to circle the vowel that makes the schwa sound in these words: **focus, liberty, allow, melon, stencil.**

Name _____

Helpful Hints

When a word has two or more syllables, one syllable is **accented,** or stressed, more than the other syllable or syllables.

In a dictionary respelling, look for an **accent mark** (**′**) *after* the accented syllable. This will help you say the word.

Marine (**mə rēn′**)   Navy (**nā′ vē**)

☆ **Read each entry word. Then read the respelling in parentheses ( ). Add an accent mark after the syllable you stress. Check a dictionary, if needed.**

1. elect   (**i lekt**)
2. budget   (**buj it**)
3. decide   (**di sīd**)
4. energy   (**en ər jē**)
5. treasure   (**trezh ər**)
6. attorney   (**ə tûr nē**)

CHALLENGE

Use a dictionary. Find two meanings for **minute**. Then find two ways to pronounce the word. Write one sentence that uses both meanings and pronunciations for **minute**.

Helpful Hint

The same word may be pronounced in different ways, depending on its meaning. The accent mark may shift to another syllable.

present (**prez′ ənt**) → going on at this time; gift
present (**pri zent′**) → to give or show

☆ **Read the sentences below. Underline the respelling of the word that best fits the meaning of the sentence. Then on the line, write the correct spelling of the word.**

7	This small tape can _____ for one hour.	(rek′ ərd)	(ri kôrd′)
8	Loyal soldiers would never _____ a wounded buddy.	(dez′ ərt)	(di zûrt′)

Read the sentences below. Underline the respelling of the word that best fits the meaning of the sentence. Then on the line, write the correct spelling of the word. Some words from the box will be used more than once.

address	content	perfect	present
progress	refuse	subject	contest

1. I remember thinking that my teacher was

    _____ in every way.   (pər fekt') (pûr' fikt)

2. She wasn't _____ unless we were
   learning something new.   (kən tent') (kon' tent)

3. She would always _____ us as "ladies
   and gentlemen," but we were only ten!   (ad' res)   (ə dres')

4. I made a remarkable amount of _____
   that year.   (prə gres') (prog' res)

5. Ms. Lane loved math, and it became

    my favorite _____.   (sub' jikt) (səb jekt')

6. She would hug anyone who would _____
   her with a homemade card or gift.   (prez' ənt) (pri zent')

7. She helped me _____ my sloppy
   handwriting.   (pər fekt') (pûr' fikt)

8. She also entered my poem in a

    poetry _____.   (kən test') (kon' test)

9. She said that she cared about the _____
   of our hearts as well as our minds.   (kən tent') (kon' tent)

10. She would never _____ to give help to
    anyone who asked for it.   (ref' ūs)   (ri fūz')

11. My education would _____ rapidly,
    thanks to her.   (prə gres') (prog' res)

LESSON 94: Accent Marks

Home Involvement Activity Use the symbols in a pronunciation key as well as accent marks to respell the names of family members. Then write the respellings on name tags to wear.

Name _____

★ **Read each group of words. Say and spell each word in bold print. Repeat the word. Then sort the words according to where you would find them in a dictionary. Write the words in the correct column below.**

- **pronunciation** key

- **respelling** of the word

- **accent** marks

- on the second **syllable**

- in alphabetical **order**

- **unfamiliar** words

- first **entry** in the book

- to **select** the best word

- reading the **definition**

- **multiple** meanings

- another **homograph**

- in **plural** form

- in a new **dictionary**

- greater **stress** here

- **between** those two words

- to **locate** the meaning

Beginning: A–I	Middle: J–Q	End: R–Z

SPELL & WRITE

Suppose a new student has joined your class. On that day, the class is working on dictionary skills. Your teacher has asked you to work as a partner with the new student. However, the student has never used a dictionary before. How would you explain how to use a dictionary?

⭐ **Plan** a set of steps that you would follow in order to find the word *welcome* in the dictionary. Write your instructions in order. Use time-order words, such as *first, next, then,* and *finally.* Use at least three of these spelling words to write your instructions.

pronunciation	respelling	accent	syllable	order
unfamiliar	entry	select	definition	multiple	homograph
plural	dictionary	stress	between	locate

_____

_____

_____

_____

_____

_____

_____

_____

_____

Writer's Tip

Check that your instructions work. Give them to a classmate to follow. Have a peer conference to find out how to improve your instructions.

Writer's Challenge

Make a list of "Dictionary Discoveries." Look through a dictionary to find interesting words for your list. Try to find words that are long, hard to pronounce, funny, unusual, or fun to draw. Define all the words. Then respell the words and add accent marks to show how to pronounce them.

Name _____

★ **Read each group of words. Fill in the circle next to the group that appears in ABC order.**

1	○ beam team scream theme ○ humble number rumble tumble ○ wrong young yeast zone	**2**	○ band bean bland brand ○ bunch crunch crash dash ○ bright slight flight mighty
3	○ sunrise noon dusk midnight ○ before during after later ○ dozen frozen nozzle sizzle	**4**	○ chance change chant chalk ○ smile smoky smooth smudge ○ elegant elect election electric
5	○ game gamble gang gallop ○ guilty guitar gulp gurgle ○ initial injury innocent index	**6**	○ Kentucky kennel Kenya khaki ○ tractor traffic towel triangle ○ quack quake quart quick
7	○ press preset present prescribe ○ able about above absorb ○ target tardy tasty taste	**8**	○ useful use usher usual ○ verb vertical video vary ○ zigzag zipper zone zoom

★ **Read each entry word in bold print. Underline the pair of guide words that would appear on the same dictionary page as the entry word.**

9. **uniform**   undo/unfold   unfortunate/union   unique/unlikely

10. **badge**   bacteria/baggage   back/bad   bag/balance

11. **officer**   odds/office   ocean/offer   offend/often

12. **summons**   suggest/sultan   sun/sunset   sulfur/sundae

13. **radio**   rabbit/radar   radiator/raid   raft/ram

14. **patrol**   patio/pattern   pause/peach   park/passage

15. **accident**   acid/acre   accent/acclaim   ache/acorn

The **United States Congress has many committees. The words in bold print give the topic of some of these committees. Circle *beginning, middle,* or *end* to tell in which part of the dictionary you would find each of these words. Use A–I for the beginning, J–Q for the middle, and R–Z for the end.**

1. **communication**   beginning   middle   end
2. **taxation**   beginning   middle   end
3. **education**   beginning   middle   end
4. **printing**   beginning   middle   end
5. **technology**   beginning   middle   end
6. **labor**   beginning   middle   end
7. **energy**   beginning   middle   end
8. **agriculture**   beginning   middle   end

Read each sentence. Underline the respelling that fits the meaning in bold print.

9	A **bear** family used to live in a cave near our farm.	(bâr)	(bîr)
10	Who shall we **elect** for class president?	(u likt′)	(i lekt′)
11	My favorite team is part of the Midwest **League**.	(lēg)	(lig)
12	Many **people** work for the city government.	(pē′ pəl)	(pe′ pül)
13	Camels are well suited for life in the **desert.**	(di zûrt′)	(dez′ ərt)
14	The County Clerk keeps **records** of births and deaths.	(rek′ ərdz)	(ri kôrdz′)
15	What is that shiny **object** in the sky?	(ob′ jikt)	(əb jekt′)
16	Is social studies your favorite **subject**?	(səb jekt′)	(sub′ jikt)

Extend & Apply

Use a dictionary to look up the meaning of these words: **document, deed, certificate.** How are the meanings the same? How are they different? Write your answers.

Name _____

Helpful Hint

Synonyms are words that have the same or nearly the same meaning.

brave—daring   bring—fetch   liberty—freedom

⭐ **Draw a line to connect each word in the first column to its synonym in the second column.**

1		2	
tired	mistake	poor	below
error	locate	language	penniless
find	divide	show	speech
separate	weary	under	exhibit

3		4	
way	following	lamp	quantity
flat	thankful	aim	light
after	manner	amount	permit
grateful	level	allow	purpose

WORK TOGETHER

Work in a group to list as many synonyms for **fast** and **slow** as you can. Compare your words with another group's list.

⭐ **One word does not belong in each group. Underline that word. Then explain on the lines below why the word does not belong in the group.**

5. work   rest   toil

_____

_____

6. make   sharpen   build

_____

_____

7. look   glance   write

_____

_____

8. paper   junk   trash

_____

_____

9. have   possess   borrow

_____

_____

10. high   tall   short

_____

_____

Unscramble the letters of the word in bold print to find a synonym for each numbered word. Then write the synonym on the line.

1. change   **ryav**   _____

2. glad   **yphpa**   _____

3. decrease   **nelsse**   _____

4. wealth   **chries**   _____

5. supply   **reodvpi**   _____

6. error   **tismkea**   _____

7. wound   **jynuri**   _____

8. occur   **phapne**   _____

Read each sentence. Then write the word from the box that is a synonym for the word in bold print.

> updates   occupations   recent   nation   difficult   neighborhood

9. A census is a count of how many people live in a **country**. _____

10. A census-taker counts the number of people and finds out their ages and **jobs**. _____

11. It is **hard** work to make an exact count. _____

12. The number of schools in a **community** is based on the census. _____

13. The government **revises** its population data after each census is done. _____

14. A census shows the **new** arrivals to a country. _____

Home Involvement Activity List as many synonyms as you can for family members. For example, list synonyms for **mother**, **father**, **child**, **grandmother**, and so on.

Name _____

Helpful Hint

Antonyms are words that have the opposite or nearly the opposite meaning.

question—answer   day—night   winter—summer

Circle the two words in each row that are antonyms of the word in bold print.

1. **trust**   assume   distrust   believe   mistrust

2. **lose**   win   fail   conquer   misplace

3. **many**   numerous   few   several   scarce

4. **before**   after   next   when   following

5. **easy**   difficult   simple   hard   uncomplicated

6. **boring**   dull   exciting   thrilling   tiresome

Replace the word in bold print with its antonym from the box.

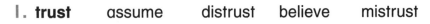

rude   damage   over   public   blame   south   win   generous

7. The politician responded to questions about her **private** life.

8. We drove **north** for ten miles, then turned west.

9. The man was **stingy** with his money.

10. The strike by city workers caused the mayor to **lose** the race.

11. A debate may **improve** the candidate's chances.

12. They were **polite** to the guest speaker.

13. The road went **under** the highway and then curved to the right.

14. Do you **forgive** me for the things I said?

CHALLENGE

Write a sensible sentence that has a pair of antonyms in it. Then write another sentence that uses *two* pairs of antonyms.

Choose the correct antonym from the box for each clue word below. Write one letter in each space. Then read down the shaded column to answer the question at the bottom.

amateur	stale	part	gentle	repair	father	cheap	lost
empty	subtract	absent	pleasure	sunset	unknown	least	

1. whole   _ _ _ _

2. mother   _ _ _ _ _ _

3. pain   _ _ _ _ _ _ _

4. full   _ _ _ _

5. famous   _ _ _ _ _ _

6. found   _ _ _ _

7. fresh   _ _ _ _

8. most   _ _ _ _

9. harsh   _ _ _ _ _ _

10. expensive   _ _ _ _

11. sunrise   _ _ _ _ _ _

12. add   _ _ _ _ _ _ _ _

13. present   _ _ _ _ _ _

14. professional   _ _ _ _ _ _ _

15. break   _ _ _ _ _ _

Question: Rowland Hill was a British civil servant who lived in the 1800s. He was interested in improving mail delivery. He introduced something that we all use today. What did Hill introduce?

Answer: _____

Home Involvement Activity What is a **philatelist**? Find out together. The post office will be glad to give you information. Do you know any **philatelists**? If so, ask them to tell you about their hobby.

Name _____

> **Helpful Hint**

Homonyms are words that sound the same but have different meanings and different spellings.

right—write   eight—ate   fourth—forth

Write the homonym from the box for each word below.

minor	maid	wait	cymbal	horse	pole
their	cruise	him	boar	mist	pail

1. made _____

2. poll _____

3. hymn _____

4. miner _____

5. bore _____

6. hoarse _____

7. weight _____

8. crews _____

9. missed _____

10. there _____

11. symbol _____

12. pale _____

Choose the homonym in parentheses ( ) that completes each sentence. Write the word on the line.

13. We usually pay sales (tacks, tax) when we buy something

    in a department store. _____

14. Postal clerks (way, weigh) letters and packages.

    _____

15. The National (Weather, Whether) Service gives

    storm warnings. _____

16. Which government agency takes care of clean

    (air, heir)? _____

> **CHALLENGE**

To, too, and **two** are homonyms. How many other sets of three homonyms can you name? Make a list.

Underline the pair of homonyms in each sentence. Then write a definition for each homonym. Check your definition in a dictionary.

1. We rode our bikes on the newly paved road.

   _____

   _____

2. Congress meets in the Capitol in our nation's capital.

   _____

   _____

3. I think that the fare for the long train ride is fair.

   _____

   _____

4. We have been putting papers in one bin and jars in another.

   _____

   _____

5. Students are not allowed to read aloud during quiet reading time.

   _____

   _____

6. They knew all about the new law for keeping dogs on a leash.

   _____

   _____

7. Will she buy the house by the stream, or the one nearer to town?

   _____

   _____

8. I guessed that my guest would stay for dinner.

   _____

   _____

Home Involvement Activity I towed the toad is a funny sentence that uses a pair of homonyms. Create five of your own funny sentences with homonym pairs.

Name _____

⭐ **Read about everybody's favorite uncle—Uncle Sam.**
Then answer the questions that follow.

Everybody's Uncle Sam

by Lester David

He is better known than any movie star, sports hero, or rock singer, even though he hasn't changed the style of his clothes in more than 100 years. He's everybody's uncle—Uncle Sam.

Uncle Sam is nothing less than the symbol for the United States of America. In fact, he is America. When a newspaper headline reads: "Uncle Sam Wins Gold Medals in Olympics," we know U.S. athletes have won.

But now for a big surprise: Uncle Sam was a real person.

During the War of 1812 against Great Britain, Sam Wilson's company supplied barrels of beef to American soldiers. In October 1812, New York Governor Daniel D. Tompkins visited Wilson's plant with a group of officials. Pointing to several barrels, one of the visitors asked the meaning of the initials "EA-US," which was stamped on top of each. One of the workers replied that "EA" stood for Elbert Anderson, who purchased meat for the Army. Then he jokingly added that the "US" meant Uncle Sam Wilson (it really stood for United States). The story spread, and soon everyone pinned the nickname to Sam Wilson.

Sam Wilson died in 1854. More than 100 years later, Congress passed a resolution saluting him as the original Uncle Sam.

"I Want You" poster by James Montgomery Flagg, first appeared in 1917, to recruit soldiers for World War I.

⭐ Reader's Response

1. **How did Uncle Sam get his name?**

2. **How does Uncle Sam stand for the United States of America?**

3. **What do you think the real Uncle Sam was like?**

You have probably seen Uncle Sam on posters, in ads, in newspapers and magazines, in parades, at fairs, and as a character in television programs and plays. In fact, the life story of Sam Wilson, the real Uncle Sam, would make a good play. Like Uncle Sam, Sam Wilson was known for his good common sense. From all over the countryside, people would ask him for advice about business, family matters, or arguments with neighbors.

Choose a problem that you face or one that you know about. How do you think Sam Wilson would have solved it? Write a dialogue in which Sam Wilson gives advice about a problem to you or another character. Use at least two of these words.

concern   improve   argument   progress   advice   leadership

suggestion   problem   solve   opinion   believe   consider

Writer's Tip

Follow the rules for writing a dialogue. Write the first name of each of your characters in capital letters followed by a colon. Do not use quotation marks.

_____

_____

_____

_____

_____

_____

_____

_____

_____

_____

Speaker's Challenge

Work with a partner to practice your dialogue. Then present it to another partner team or to a small group. Speak in the voice that you think Sam Wilson or Uncle Sam would have used.

Name _____

In a dictionary, you look up a word to learn its meaning. In a **thesaurus,** you look up a word to find its synonyms, or words with almost the same meaning. Sometimes, antonyms (*ant*), words with opposite meanings, are given, too.

Read the thesaurus entry below for the word *run*. You would look up *run* in the same way that you would look up a word in the dictionary. Notice that this thesaurus entry gives synonyms and antonyms.

run [*v*] bolt, bound, bustle, dart, dash, gallop, jog, rush, scramble, scurry, sprint, trot; *Ant* crawl, stand, walk

Choose a synonym or an antonym for *run* that best fits the movement in each picture. Use the words from the thesaurus entry above.

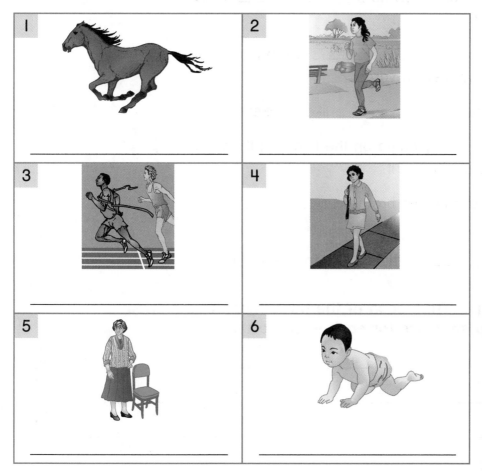

1. _____

2. _____

3. _____

4. _____

5. _____

6. _____

WORD STRATEGY

A **thesaurus** can help you find the exact word to use in your writing. Write a sentence for each of these synonyms for *small*.

    little
    puny
    teeny

Use the best synonym for the entry word in bold print to complete each sentence. Choose a word from the three thesaurus entries below.

| **laugh** [v] cackle, chuckle, giggle, guffaw, hoot, snort, snicker | **throw** [v] chuck, flick, fling, heave, hurl, lob, pitch, toss | **write** [v] compose, draft, enter, jot down, mark, print, scrawl, scribble |

1. I gave a loud _____ when the bucket fell on the clown's head.

2. The strong man lifts the heavy rock and _____ it aside.

3. I've just _____ a note to my mother.

4. The trainer had me _____ the ball to the excited puppy.

5. We began to _____ when the funny music began.

6. How old was Mozart when he _____ that piece of music?

7. The Olympic athlete _____ the ball high over the fence into my friend's yard.

8. We all started to _____ like chickens.

9. I _____ my name on the line and then neatly wrote my signature below it.

10. I can't read what my little brother _____ on the paper.

11. Please _____ that litter into the trash can.

Choose one synonym from each of the three thesaurus entries above. Write a sentence for each word you pick.

12. _____

13. _____

14. _____

Home Involvement Activity Become a "family thesaurus." Together, list as many synonyms as you can for the words **good** and **bad**.

Name _____

Helpful Hint

A **thesaurus** lists synonyms and antonyms. It can help you use more interesting and more exact words in your writing. Most thesauruses are arranged in **ABC order** like a dictionary.

The box below has synonyms from a thesaurus for the words *big*, *happy*, and *small*. Sort the words by their meaning. Write each word in the correct column.

content   gigantic   great   little   roomy   tiny   vast   overjoyed

enormous   wee   delighted   cheerful   petite   teeny   thrilled

1 **big**	2 **happy**	3 **small**
_____	_____	_____
_____	_____	_____
_____	_____	_____
_____	_____	_____
_____	_____	_____

Rank each set of words from *least* to *most*. Write the words in the correct order on the lines below.

4. from *least* angry to *most* angry: annoyed, furious, angry

_____

5. from *least* hot to *most* hot: sizzling, hot, warm

_____

6. from *least* noisy to *most* noisy: thunderous, loud, faint

_____

CHALLENGE

Read the words in the **happy** column above. Rank them from *least* happy to *most* happy.

Replace each word in bold print with a more exact word from the box.

tiny	roomy	undersized	gigantic	pleased
stunted	delighted	vast	bulky	ecstatic

1. The national park had a **big** number of acres. _____

2. I needed both arms to carry the **big** package. _____

3. The **big** bedroom could hold a chair, two dressers, a desk, and a bed. _____

4. The whale is the largest mammal on earth. It is **big**! _____

5. A **small** bug crawled across the paper. _____

6. The **small** wrestler was no match for his opponent. _____

7. The plant was **small** because it didn't get enough water and light. _____

8. We were **happy** when our candidate finally won. _____

9. She was **happy** with the voting results but not thrilled. _____

10. The audience was **happy** to hear her speech. _____

Former Texas representative Barbara Jordan speaking at the Democratic National Convention in 1992.

Home Involvement Activity Choose five of the words in the box at the top to describe something or someone in your home.

Name _____

Read each group of words. Say and spell each word in bold print. Repeat the word. Then sort the words. In the chart below, write two pairs of synonyms, three pairs of antonyms, and three pairs of homonyms.

- from another **country**
- the **fare** for the bus
- a **polite** smile
- too long to **wait**
- sang a **gentle** lullaby
- made a **mistake**
- did the **right** thing
- go to **private** school
- **error** in judgment
- to **write** a speech
- **public** transportation
- **fair** weather

- gaining **weight**
- **rude** remarks
- **harsh** punishment
- a free **nation**

Synonyms	Antonyms	Homonyms

Every few years, the people of the United States get a chance to vote for the candidate of their choice. These candidates use advertisements, public appearances, debates, and speeches to get their points across to the voters.

Imagine that you are running for the office of class president. Write a speech that will persuade your classmates to vote for you. Give three strong reasons. Use at least one pair of synonyms, one pair of antonyms, or one pair of homonyms from the box below.

country fare polite wait gentle mistake right private

error write public fair weight rude harsh nation

Writer's Tip

Read your speech again. Look in a thesaurus to replace an ordinary word with a more exact synonym.

Speaker's Challenge

Use note cards to jot down the important points of your speech. Practice using your note cards before giving your speech to the class.

Your Vote Counts

Name _____

Read each pair of words. Write *S* if the words are synonyms. Write *A* if the words are antonyms. Write *H* if the words are homonyms.

1. below—under _____
2. weight—wait _____
3. mist—missed _____
4. wealth—riches _____
5. tall—lofty _____
6. vast—big _____
7. moist—dry _____
8. add—subtract _____
9. part—whole _____
10. hoarse—horse _____
11. pole—poll _____
12. stale—fresh _____
13. permit—allow _____
14. little—tiny _____
15. aloud—allowed _____
16. weather—whether _____
17. many—few _____
18. public—private _____
19. pitch—fling _____
20. boring—thrilling _____
21. tacks—tax _____
22. throw—toss _____

The box below has synonyms for the words *laugh* and *write*. Sort the words by their meaning. Write each word in the correct column.

cackle	compose	chuckle	draft
giggle	guffaw	scribble	jot down

23 **Words for *laugh***	24 **Words for *write***
_____	_____
_____	_____
_____	_____
_____	_____

CHALLENGE

Replace the word in bold print with both a synonym and an antonym.

quiet music
fair weather
good grades

Underline the synonym for each word in bold print.

1. **shut** the gate   paint   <u>close</u>   fix

2. **stroll** in the park   sleep   jog   <u>walk</u>

3. unknown **quantity**   <u>amount</u>   person   quality

4. **aid** for flood victims   sorrow   food   <u>help</u>

5. the day **after** the election   before   of   <u>following</u>

6. **glance** out the window   throw   <u>look</u>   call

Underline the antonym for each word in bold print.

7. likes **winter** sports   team   fall   <u>summer</u>

8. **several** highways   many   <u>few</u>   a lot of

9. **easy** to understand   simple   <u>hard</u>   smart

10. **over** the speed limit   top   obey   <u>under</u>

11. **scurries** away   dashes   jogs   <u>crawls</u>

Underline the correct homonym from the homonym pair in the box to complete each sentence. Then write the word on the line.

| bin/been   knew/new   buy/by |

12. Has your group ever _____ to Mount Rushmore?

13. I _____ someone who worked there.

14. I asked her to _____ me carved stone bookends from the gift shop.

Extend & Apply

Use a thesaurus to revise sentences 12–14. Change one word in each sentence. Choose a word that is more interesting or exact.

Mount Rushmore

Name _____

Helpful Hint

Language changes all the time as people use it. Sometimes, long words get shortened so that they are easier to say and spell. These shorter forms are called **clipped words.**

gasoline→**gas**   laboratory→**lab**

 Draw a line to match each clipped word in Column *A* with the long form of that word in Column *B*. Write the long form of the word on the line.

	A	**B**
_____	1. auto	**a.** bicycle
_____	2. plane	**b.** mathematics
_____	3. vet	**c.** influenza
_____	4. flu	**d.** telephone
_____	5. gym	**e.** gymnasium
_____	6. bike	**f.** veterinarian
_____	7. math	**g.** automobile
_____	8. phone	**h.** airplane

Read each sentence. Replace the word in bold print with the clipped word in the box. Write the clipped word on the line.

pro	copter	sub	exam

9. The class is taking a science **examination**. _____

10. Our teacher was once a **professional** bowler. _____

11. He also served on a **submarine** in the Navy. _____

12. Mr. Vargas flies a **helicopter,** too. _____

CHALLENGE

Write the long form of each of these clipped words. Use a dictionary to help you.

zoo

ad

cell phone

Helpful Hint

Language also changes when new words are added. **Blended words** are new words that are formed by combining two words. As a result, some letters are dropped.

smoke + fog = smog

Complete each sentence. Combine the letters in bold print in the two words to form one blended word.

1. If you blend **tw**ist + wh**irl**, you get _____.

2. If you blend **fl**utter + **hurry**, you get _____.

3. If you blend **c**hunk + **lump**, you get _____.

4. If you blend **fl**ame + gl**are**, you get _____.

5. If you blend **slo**p + slu**sh**, you get _____.

6. If you blend **br**eakfast + **l**unch, you get _____.

7. If you blend **gl**eam + sh**immer**, you get _____.

8. If you blend **tele**vision + mara**thon**, you get _____.

9. If you blend **mo**tor + ho**tel**, you get _____.

10. If you blend **cam**era + re**corder**, you get _____.

Write one of the blended words from above to complete each sentence.

11. My sister taught me how to _____ a baton.

12. On clear nights, you can see the faint _____ of faraway stars.

13. The captain lit a signal _____ to call for help.

14. The _____ for the hospital raised more than $2 million.

15. After the heavy rain, we had to _____ through deep mud.

16. There was a _____ of excitement when the mayor arrived.

LESSON 105: Clipped Words and Blended Words

Home Involvement Activity You may have a fax machine or a modem at home. **Fax** is a clipped word. **Modem** is a blended word. Work together to find out how each word was formed.

Name _____

Each of the words in the box has been borrowed from another language. Write the correct word from the box to complete each sentence. Begin the word with a capital letter.

ukulele	library	pajamas	menu
pretzel	moccasin	thesaurus	umbrella

1. _____ is an Algonquian word for a soft leather slipper.

2. _____ is a Hindi word for clothes for sleeping.

3. _____ is a French word for the list of foods at a restaurant.

4. _____ is a German word for a salty, twisted bread snack.

5. _____ is a Greek word for a book of synonyms and antonyms.

6. _____ is a Hawaiian word for a small guitarlike instrument.

7. _____ is an Italian word for something that protects you in the rain.

8. _____ is a Latin word for a place where books are kept.

CHALLENGE

Match each food with the language from which it was borrowed:

bagel   Taino
potato   Bantu
gumbo   Yiddish

Learn more about these words and languages by checking the dictionary.

Solve this crossword puzzle that uses borrowed words. All answers appear in the Word Bank. The language from which each word was borrowed appears in the Word Bank, too.

Across

2. machine that can do some of the things a human can do
4. thick tropical forest
8. detective
9. collection of articles, printed each week or month
12. couch
13. grade before first grade
14. opposite of war
16. instrument with a keyboard
17. small, furry rodent pet
18. pale tan color

Down

1. sour yellow fruit
3. circus swing
4. type of American music
5. to rub away pencil marks
6. fish used in sandwiches
7. chess piece
10. child without parents
11. prehistoric animal: woolly _____
13. yellowish-brown cloth used for army uniforms
15. chubby angel child with wings

Word Bank

Arabic: lemon, magazine, sofa

Creole: jazz

Czech: robot

French: beige, trapeze

German: hamster, kindergarten

Greek: orphan, bishop

Hebrew: cherub

Hindi: jungle, khaki

Icelandic: sleuth

Italian: piano

Latin: erase, peace

Russian: mammoth

Spanish: tuna

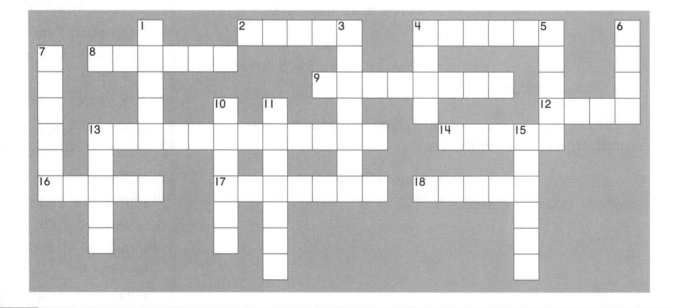

Home Involvement Activity Many foods that people eat in the United States have names that are borrowed from other languages, such as **waffle, taco,** and **spaghetti.** Work together to list foods that have borrowed names.

Name _____

Helpful Hint

An **idiomatic expression** (or **idiom**) is a phrase that means something different from what it seems to mean. Idiomatic expressions are part of everyday speech.

The social studies test was **a piece of cake.**
means The social studies test was *very easy.*

Do you **get the picture?**
means Do you *understand*?

★ **Each numbered sentence has an idiom in bold print. Circle the letter of the answer that means the same thing as the sentence that has the idiom.**

1. The young actor **stole the show**.
   a. The young actor took a show that didn't belong to him.
   b. The young actor got more attention than the other performers.
   c. The young actor stole the script.

2. I **got cold feet** when it was my turn to speak.
   a. I was afraid to speak when my turn came.
   b. My feet got cold when I spoke.
   c. I showed some cold feet with my speech.

3. Dana stands **head and shoulders above** the other students.
   a. Dana is taller than the other students.
   b. Dana's marks or behavior is better than that of the other students.
   c. Dana's abilities as an acrobat are better than those of the other students.

4. **Money burns a hole in my pocket.**
   a. I use money that is so hot that it burns my pockets.
   b. I wear pants with pockets that easily burn.
   c. I quickly spend any money I get.

CHALLENGE

Draw a funny cartoon to illustrate one of the idiomatic expressions on this page—or illustrate another idiom that you think would make a funny cartoon.

Each sentence at the left has an idiom in bold print. Draw a line to connect the sentence with the idiom to the sentence at the right that means the same thing.

1. They are not out **of the woods yet.**

2. They didn't **know the ropes.**

3. They are all **in the same boat.**

4. He **got up on the wrong side of the bed.**

5. He will **drop me a line.**

6. They **hit the roof** when he asked to borrow the car.

7. I was **down in the dumps.**

8. Everything you say to him **goes in one ear and out the other.**

9. I **spent an arm and a leg** on a fan.

10. He told me to **keep it under my hat.**

a. They didn't know how things worked.

b. They all face the same situation.

c. He will write to me.

d. They are not yet free of trouble.

e. He was in a bad mood.

f. He said I should keep it a secret.

g. I bought a very expensive fan.

h. I was unhappy.

i. Everything you say goes through his mind without making an impression.

j. They became angry when he asked to borrow the car.

Choose four idiomatic expressions from above. Use each idiom in a sentence that shows its meaning.

11. _____

_____

12. _____

_____

13. _____

_____

14. _____

_____

Home Involvement Activity Interview an older family member or a neighbor. Ask the person to tell you some idiomatic expressions that he or she used to hear but doesn't hear anymore. Find out what these expressions mean.

Name _____

Word analogies show how words and ideas are related.
            High is to **low** as **big** is to **small**.
THINK: **High** and **low** are *opposites*. **Big** and **small**
            are *opposites*. The words in both pairs show
            a relationship. Both are *antonyms*.

You can also write the analogy like this:
            high : low :: big : small

Here are some other ways that pairs of words are related:

They are *synonyms*.   **Begin** is to **start** as
                                        stop is to **halt**.

They show *cause and effect*.   **Hungry** is to **eat** as
                                        tired is to **rest**.

They show *parts of a whole*.   **toe : foot :: room : house**
They show how objects
are *used*.   **pencil : write :: knife : cut**

**Read each word analogy. Write how the words in both pairs
   are related. Choose from these words or word pairs:
   *synonyms, antonyms, cause/effect, part/whole, object/use.***

1. *Most* is to *least* as *new* is to *old*.

   _____

2. *Hard* is to *difficult* as *careful* is to *cautious*.

   _____

3. *Finger* is to *hand* as *page* is to *book*.

   _____

4. *Study* is to *learn* as *practice* is to *improve*.

   _____

5. *Couch* is to *sit* as *bed* is to *sleep*.

   _____

CHALLENGE

Make up a word
analogy using
either synonyms
or antonyms.
Leave out the last
word. Have a
friend complete
your analogy.

Circle the letter of the word that completes each analogy.
Then write the word on the line.

1. *Lost* is to *found* as *loose* is to

_____

a. lively
b. tight
c. long
d. missing

2. *Foot* is to *leg* as *nose* is to

_____

a. lips
b. eyes
c. face
d. smell

3. *Glass* is to *drink* as *fork* is to

_____

a. spoon
b. eat
c. cut
d. plate

4. *Story* is to *tale* as *idea* is to

_____

a. book
b. poem
c. secret
d. thought

5. *Wet* is to *dry* as *tame* is to

_____

a. wild
b. wetter
c. team
d. rain

6. *Winning* is to *trophy* as *crime* is to

_____

a. criminal
b. reward
c. victory
d. punishment

7. hero : villain :: friend :

_____

a. pal
b. enemy
c. classmate
d. cousin

8. thin : slender :: injury :

_____

a. thick
b. wound
c. slim
d. doctor

9. needle : sew :: broom :

_____

a. sweep
b. paint
c. wash
d. shovel

10. finger : hand :: classroom :

_____

a. city
b. state
c. school
d. house

Betsy Ross (1756–1832)
sewing the first American flag

LESSON 108: Word Analogies

Home Involvement Activity Solve this word analogy:
Kitchen is to house as neighborhood is to _____.
Explain your answer. Work together to make up other
analogies that you can have fun solving.

Name _____

⭐ **Read about a special kind of government worker.
Then answer the questions that follow.**

Park Rangers

They wear green and khaki uniforms and unusual hats. They also wear name tags and badges. They work in some of the most beautiful, exciting, and important places in the United States. These government workers care about the past, the present, and the future. They value the environment. They listen and also teach. These men and women lead tours and hikes, and give directions. Who are these people? Can you guess? They are our nation's park rangers.

Park rangers work for the National Parks Service (NPS). The National Parks Service has an important job. It must protect America's natural resources. The Service cares for land that our government owns. It cares for national parks like the Grand Canyon. It takes care of historical sites like Valley Forge. It cares for national monuments like the Statue of Liberty.

It takes a large staff to care for so many places. Our many park rangers come from all fifty states. They learn all about the park or site. Some may even live within the park grounds. These rangers share their knowledge of our nation's beauty and history with anyone who is lucky enough to visit one of these wonderful sites.

Park ranger with tourists at the Grand Canyon

💥 📖 Reader's Response

1. **What does a park ranger do?**

2. **What is the main idea of this selection? Give three details that support the main idea.**

3. **Would you like to be a park ranger? If so, where would you like to work?**

LESSON 109: Connecting Reading and Writing
Comprehension—Main Idea and Details;
Synthesize

221

Most park rangers enjoy their jobs. They get to serve their country in important ways. They meet people from the United States and from all over the world. They get an inside look at some of our national treasures. Many park rangers even get to live among nature.

Choose a national park or a historical site or monument. Imagine that you are applying for the job of park ranger there. Write notes for a job application letter. Tell why you would be right for the job. Use at least two of these words.

| public | history | service | information | outdoors | directions |
| nature | leadership | communicate | site | uniform | friendly |

The Place: _____

_____

The Job: _____

_____

Your Experience: _____

_____

_____

Your Skills and Interests: _____

_____

_____

_____

Writer's Tip

Read some "help-wanted" ads in the newspaper to see the kinds of details to include.

Speaker's Challenge

Imagine that you are being interviewed for the job of park ranger. Work with a partner to role-play the job interview. Make a list of the questions beforehand and think about the answers. Then role-play your interview for another partner team.

Name _____

Is it a clipped word or a blended word? Underline your answer. Then write the word or words that make up the clipped or blended word.

1. photo   clipped word   blended word _____

2. teen   clipped word   blended word _____

3. brunch   clipped word   blended word _____

4. lab   clipped word   blended word _____

5. smog   clipped word   blended word _____

6. vet   clipped word   blended word _____

7. motel   clipped word   blended word _____

8. champ   clipped word   blended word _____

9. bike   clipped word   blended word _____

10. fax   clipped word   blended word _____

Each sentence below has an idiom in bold print. Circle the letter of the answer that means the same thing as the sentence that has the idiom.

11. Our homework was **a piece of cake.**
    a. Our homework was very easy.
    b. Our homework was to bake a cake.
    c. Our homework was to eat a piece of cake.

12. Do you **get the picture?**
    a. Do you get the prize?
    b. Do you have to buy the painting?
    c. Do you understand?

13. Some computers **cost an arm and a leg.**
    a. Some computers have hands and feet.
    b. Some computers cost a great deal of money.
    c. Some computers can hurt your arms and legs.

REVIEW & ASSESS

Read the passage. Then answer the questions that follow.

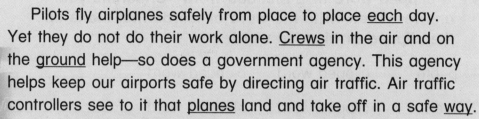

Pilots fly airplanes safely from place to place <u>each</u> day. Yet they do not do their work alone. <u>Crews</u> in the air and on the <u>ground</u> help—so does a government agency. This agency helps keep our airports safe by directing air traffic. Air traffic controllers see to it that <u>planes</u> land and take off in a safe <u>way</u>.

Air traffic controllers work for the Department of Transportation. Their job can be stressful at busy times or in bad weather. They must <u>act</u> quickly if there is a problem. Anyone who has ever flown can thank these important government workers.

⭐ **Read the passage again to answer these questions. Circle the letter of the correct answer.**

1. The correct respelling for <u>each</u> is
   a. ēch.
   b. ech.
   c. əch.
   d. əsh.

2. A homonym for <u>crews</u> is
   a. teams.
   b. cruise.
   c. staff.
   d. characters.

3. The best antonym for <u>ground</u> in the passage is
   a. chopped up.
   b. air.
   c. land.
   d. soil.

4. <u>Planes</u> is a clipped word for
   a. plains.
   b. planets.
   c. planetariums.
   d. airplanes.

5. The best synonym for <u>way</u> is
   a. thrust.
   b. whey.
   c. weigh.
   d. manner.

6. The closest meaning of <u>act</u> is
   a. rehearse.
   b. call.
   c. do something.
   d. turn on the radio.

Extend & Apply

Air traffic controllers report to the **FAA**. Use a dictionary or an encyclopedia to find out what **FAA** stands for.